THE CLASSIC AMERICAN QUILT COLLECTION™

ONE PATCH

Edited by
Karen Costello Soltys

 Rodale Press, Emmaus, Pennsylvania

OUR MISSION

We publish books that empower people's lives.

RODALE BOOKS

ONE PATCH EDITORIAL STAFF

Editor: *Karen Costello Soltys*

Technical Writer: *Janet Wickell*

Quilt Scout: *Bettina Havig*

Cover and Interior Designer: *Denise M. Shade*

Book Layout: *Tanya L. Lipinski*

Photographer: *Mitch Mandel*

Illustrators: *Mario Ferro and Jackie Walsh*

Studio Manager: *Leslie Keefe*

Copy Editor: *Carolyn Mandarano*

Administrative Assistance: *Stephanie Wenner*

Manufacturing Coordinator: *Jodi Schaffer*

RODALE BOOKS

Editorial Director, Home and Garden: *Margaret Lydic Balitas*

Managing Editor, Quilt Books: *Suzanne Nelson*

Art Director, Home and Garden: *Michael Mandarano*

Associate Art Director, Home and Garden: *Mary Ellen Fanelli*

Copy Director, Home and Garden: *Dolores Plikaitis*

Office Manager, Home and Garden: *Karen Earl-Braymer*

Editor-in-Chief: *William Gottlieb*

If you have any questions or comments concerning this book, please write to:
Rodale Press, Inc.
Book Readers' Service
33 East Minor Street
Emmaus, PA 18098

Library of Congress Cataloging-in-Publication Data

Classic American quilt collection. One patch /
edited by Karen Costello Soltys.
p. cm.
ISBN 0–87596–684–5 (hardcover : alk. paper)
1. Patchwork—United States—Patterns.
2. Quilting—United States—Patterns. 3. Patchwork quilts—United States. I. Soltys, Karen Costello.
TT835.C592   1995
746.46—dc20   95–18466

Distributed in the book trade by St. Martin's Press

2 4 6 8 10 9 7 5 3 1   hardcover

CONTENTS

ACKNOWLEDGMENTS

Natural Balance, made by Shelly Burge of Lincoln, Nebraska. Natural Balance has been juried in several quilt shows across the country, and it has won several awards, including First Place in scrap quilts at Shelly's home guild show, the Omaha Quilters Guild annual show. Shelly is also a founding member of the Nebraska State Quilt Guild.

Mountain Mirage, made by Kathryn Kuhn of Monument, Colorado. Kathryn is a member of her local quilt guild, Piecing Partners, and the Colorado Quilt Council. Her quilt first appeared in *Quilter's Newsletter Magazine* in February 1988 and was shown at Jinny Beyer's Hilton Head, South Carolina, seminar. Kathryn coauthored the book *Appliqué the Easy Way.*

6 ÷ 3 = 5, by Edith Zimmer of San Diego, California. Edith is an award-winning quilter, quilting teacher, and lecturer. The pentagon shape in her One Patch quilt was derived from Jinny Beyer's book *The Scraplook.* Edith had never seen a quilt pieced from a pentagon, so she devised the color-spectrum diagonal setting for a unique quilt.

Grandmother's Flower Garden, owned by Kathryn Jones of Marshall, Missouri. This quilt was pieced by Lelia Poindexter, Kathryn's great-grandmother, in 1938-39 and hand quilted by Kathryn in 1994. Kathryn is one of the founders of the Country Patchwork Quilters Guild. She is also a member of the Booneslick Trail Quilter's Guild.

Damon's Diamond Delight, made by Cherry Schorfheide of Bolivar, Missouri. Cherry has been quilting for 15 years. Her quilt, named for her son, has won a variety of awards, including the *Better Homes and Gardens* Grand Prize in patchwork at the AIQA Quilt Show in Houston in 1990.

Barn Raising Pinwheels, pieced by Barbara Berliner of Columbia, Missouri, and machine quilted by Cathy Sexton. Barbara made this quilt for her son, Matthew. She has been quilting for over 10 years and is an active member of the Booneslick Trail Quilters Guild. Her quilt design is a variation of a pattern that originally appeared in *Quiltmaker* No. 23 called Give and Take.

Charming Spools, made by Phyllis Klein of Warwick, New York. Phyllis is an active quilter and guild member. She has organized quilt shows, restored antique quilts, taught numerous classes, and collected fabrics from across the country and abroad. In addition to her commitments to quilting organizations, Phyllis has found time to make over 100 quilts since her first foray into quilting in 1974.

Thousand Pyramids, made by Bettina Havig of Columbia, Missouri. Bettina's traditional One Patch quilt was pieced and quilted entirely by hand and has appeared in *Lady's Circle Patchwork Quilts.* Bettina, who has been quilting since 1970, was the director of the Missouri Heritage Quilt Project, is a board member of the Quilt Conservancy, and is a member of the American Quilt Study Group, the Booneslick Trail Quilter's Guild, and the Missouri State Quilters Guild.

Simply Charming, made by Edith Zimmer of San Diego, California. This quilt's unique setting combines traditional Baby Blocks with Eight-Pointed Stars in an unusual design and appeared in the January 1988 issue of *Quilter's Newsletter Magazine.*

Charmed Ogee, made by Julia Zgliniec of Poway, California. Julia is a quiltmaker, instructor, and quilt appraiser certified by the American Quilter's Society. Julia's quilts have appeared in numerous shows across the country. She designs fabrics for South Sea Imports, founded Quilt San Diego, is a member of the American Quilt Study Group, and works on the Visions shows held in California.

Evening at the Lily Pond, made by Kathryn Kuhn. Kathryn's fascination with hexagon variations led her to make both of her charm quilts that appear in this book. Like Mountain Mirage, this quilt was shown at Jinny Beyer's Hilton Head, South Carolina, seminar.

Tumbling Blocks, made by Jacqueline Chace of Jefferson City, Missouri. Jacqueline has been quilting for nine years. She has gained inspiration from members of her first guild, the Booneslick Trail Quilter's Guild, as well as from acquaintances made while working at the Great American Quilt Factory in Colorado. Jacqueline was also inspired by visiting lecturer Jinny Beyer.

INTRODUCTION

But let no one imagine that these all-over one-patch quilts were easy to design.
Such quilts must be comprehended in their entirety rather than by patches or blocks,
and therefore they require the eye of a true artist both as regards (to) color and form.
—Ruth Finley, *Old Patchwork Quilts and the Women Who Made Them*

One Patch quilts. The mere name sounds easy. It seems that nothing could be simpler than sewing bits and pieces of scraps—all the same shape, no less—into a quilt. But, as Ruth Finley stated in her book in 1929, depending on the shape of the patch you choose, a One Patch quilt can be a bit tricky to design.

That's why we're delighted to share 12 wonderful One Patch quilts with you, each expertly designed to provide tremendous visual impact. So with the color and form aspects taken care of by our acknowledged quiltmakers, let's get down to basics. Just what is a One Patch quilt?

One Patch quilts and charm quilts are quite often one and the same—a quilt pieced entirely from just one shape that is cut from many different fabrics, using each fabric only once. You'll find, however, that a One Patch doesn't have to be a charm quilt. Take a look at the cheery yellow Grandmother's Flower Garden quilt on page 28, and you'll see that it's made entirely of hexagons, yet the bright yellow solid fabric is repeated throughout the quilt to connect the flowers.

With that said, you'll find a fair share of charm quilts in this volume. You'll even find One Patch quilts that aren't 100 percent authentic One Patch quilts. In our quest to find a sparkling variety of color, shapes, and designs, we fell in love with several quilts that had exquisite borders. And to put a straight-edged border on irregular-shaped quilt sides, you have to add half and quarter pieces to even out the edges. But they're close enough to argue their One Patch status, and we wouldn't have wanted you to miss out on these wonderful patchwork examples.

You'll find projects of all sizes, color schemes, and skill levels. Project directions also provide variety, ranging from machine piecing to English paper piecing, with lots of tips for success using any method.

To help you choose which project to make first, we've included our usual skill level ratings. You'll find that each project is rated Easy, Intermediate, Advanced, or Challenging. These are merely our guides that indicate the complexity of the quilt as compared to the other quilts in this book. If you are a confident beginner, you may feel completely at ease working on one of the Intermediate-level projects, so don't let a skill rating intimidate you.

In addition to the detailed project directions, One Patch Basics, beginning on page 104, is packed with information on working with color values and scraps to recreate spectacular One Patch quilts. So if you are ready to take on the challenge of designing your own One Patch color scheme or quilt layout, you'll find helpful information, suggestions, and tips that go beyond the step-by-step assembly directions.

If you've never made a charm or One Patch quilt, you're in for a treat. Some shapes may be a bit more challenging than others. But whichever shape you make your one template, you're bound to have fun collecting fabrics, arranging and rearranging your pieces, and stitching them all together, one piece at a time. Before you get started, you might want to organize a scrap fabric swap with your friends. One of the best things about making a One Patch quilt is that you get to work with lots and lots of fabrics!

Karen Soltys

Karen Costello Soltys

One Patch
Projects

Natural Balance

Skill Level: *Easy*

*N*atural Balance *is an original quilt design by Shelly Burge of Lincoln, Nebraska. Shelly discovered her off-kilter Four Patch design while drafting a kaleidoscope block. The Four Patch block is actually quite simple to piece, but the color placement is the key to making the dark and light pinwheels appear. Another important element in this wallhanging or lap quilt is the curved line quilting, which makes the pinwheels dance and twirl across the quilt top.*

BEFORE YOU BEGIN

The blocks in this charm quilt are quite easy to make, since all seams are straight lines and require no setting in. Each block is simply a Four Patch that is slightly askew.

The challenging part of assembling the quilt is the color placement. The quiltmaker carefully arranged the color and value so that the Four Patch blocks form spinning pinwheels in the quilt center and a jagged border surrounding them. These two different effects are made with the same basic block; only the color placement is different.

CHOOSING FABRICS

If you are a fabric collector, coming up with 624 different fabrics to make this charm quilt may be no problem. This quiltmaker drew upon her stash of fabrics that she collected over many years.

To expand your own fabric collection, organize a fabric swap with quilting friends or guild members. Assortments of precut squares and fat quarters are available from some quilt shops or mail-order sources, and these are easy and relatively inexpensive ways to accumulate fabric for a scrap quilt.

Quilt Sizes		
	Lap (shown)	Queen
Finished Quilt Size	60½" × 65½"	95½" × 100½"
Finished Block Size	5"	5"
Total Number of Blocks	156	380
Block 1	72	240
Block 2	42	70
Block 3	17	31
Block 4	17	31
Block 5	4	4
Block 6	4	4

Materials		
	Lap	Queen
Assorted dark prints	3 yards	7⅜ yards
Assorted medium prints	2 yards	5¾ yards
Assorted light prints	2 yards	3 yards
Backing	4¼ yards	8¾ yards
Batting	69" × 74"	104" × 109"
Binding	⅝ yard	⅞ yard

NOTE: *Yardages are estimates, based on using scraps that measure at least 3¼ × 4½ inches.*

Each pinwheel grouping is pieced from the same color and value—not a small feat considering how many block corners had to coordinate to make this

Cutting Chart

Fabric	Used For	Piece	Number to Cut	
			Lap	Queen
Dark prints	Blocks 1, 2, 3, 4, 5, 6	A	274	694
Medium prints	Blocks 1, 3, 4, 6	A	182	546
Light prints	Blocks 2, 3, 4, 5, 6	A	168	280

possible. So, if you plan to include red, for example, you will need several different red prints that are all similar in value, such as brick reds, burgundys, or bright reds.

To make a quilt similar to the one shown, choose a large variety of fabrics in three different color values—dark, medium, and light. For more information about color value, refer to page 106. You might decide to design your own version of Natural Balance, perhaps assembling it in a monochromatic layout. For instance, you could use three different values of one color family, such as light, medium, and dark blue, to assemble the blocks. Or you may choose to make your quilt in colors and values with even more contrast than the one shown, such as black, yellow, and red. Photocopy the **Color Plan** on page 9, and use crayons or colored pencils to have fun creating your own design.

CUTTING

All pieces for this quilt are cut using pattern piece A on page 8. Construct a durable template from the pattern, as you will need to cut hundreds of pieces with this one template. The pattern piece includes ¼-inch seam allowances. Refer to the Cutting Chart for the number of pieces you need to cut from each color value. Note that piece A is not symmetrical. Position the template right side up on the wrong side of the fabric for tracing and cutting the fabric. For more information about making and using templates, see page 116.

Note: Cut and piece one sample block before cutting all the fabric for the quilt.

PIECING THE BLOCKS

The entire quilt is made from skewed Four Patch blocks, and each block is constructed in the same manner. The only difference between the blocks is the color placement within the blocks. Six different color value arrangements are used and are labeled Blocks 1 through 6. Refer to the Quilt Sizes chart on page 3 for the number of each type of block required for your quilt size.

Step 1. Block 1, as shown in the **Block Diagram,** is used throughout the center of the quilt. When multiple blocks are positioned as shown in **Diagram 1,** dark and medium pinwheels are formed where blocks meet. For more control over the final design, lay out all pieces before sewing any together, using the photograph on page 2 or the **Quilt Diagram** on page 7 as a reference for color placement.

Block Diagram

Medium pinwheel   Dark and medium
is formed   pinwheels appear

Diagram 1

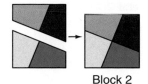

Block 2

Diagram 4

Step 6. Sew two light A pieces together to form half of Block 3. Then sew together a medium and dark piece, as shown in **Diagram 5.** Press the adjoining seams in opposite directions and sew the block halves together. Press the long seam toward the darker fabrics. Repeat to make the required number of Block 3 for your quilt size.

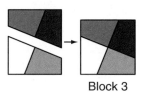

Block 3

Diagram 5

Step 7. Block 4 is also made of two light, one medium, and one dark piece; however, the position of the medium and dark pieces are reversed from those in Block 3. Assemble the block halves, as shown in **Diagram 6.** Press the adjoining seams in opposite directions and sew the block halves together. Press the long seam toward the darker fabrics. Repeat until you've assembled the required number of Block 4 for your quilt size.

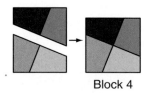

Block 4

Diagram 6

Step 8. Block 5 is made of three dark pieces and one light piece. Sew the pieces together, as shown in **Diagram 7** on page 6. Press adjoining seams in opposite directions and sew the block halves together. Press the long seam toward the two darker fabrics. Make four of Block 5 for either size quilt.

Step 2. To make Block 1, sew a dark A piece to a medium A piece, as shown in **Diagram 2.** Press the seam toward the dark piece.

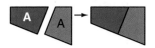

Diagram 2

Step 3. Repeat, making an identical unit. With right sides together, align the diagonal sides of the two units, matching the center seam intersections. Sew the two units together, as shown in **Diagram 3.** Press the seam to one side.

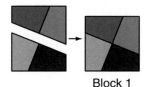

Block 1

Diagram 3

Step 4. Repeat Steps 2 and 3 to assemble the total number of Block 1 required for your quilt.

Step 5. To make Block 2 for the border of the quilt, assemble the two block halves from a light and dark A, as shown in **Diagram 4.** Press the seams in opposite directions, and sew the block halves together. Press the long seam to one side. Repeat until you've assembled the required number of Block 2 for your quilt size.

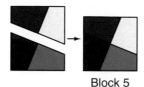

Block 5

Diagram 7

Step 9. For Block 6, you will need three light pieces and one medium or one dark piece. Assemble the two block halves, as shown in **Diagram 8.** Press the adjoining seams in opposite directions and sew the block halves together. Press the long seam to one side. Make four of Block 6 for either size quilt—two blocks with a medium piece and two blocks with a dark piece.

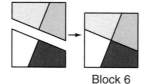

Block 6

Diagram 8

ASSEMBLING THE QUILT TOP

Step 1. Use a design wall or other flat surface to arrange your quilt blocks into rows, as shown in the **Partial Assembly Diagram.** If you are making the lap quilt, also refer to **Diagram 9** for an easy placement reference for each block type. Make sure you have each block positioned as shown, or you will not have pinwheels where your blocks connect. The grid in **Diagram 10** shows placement of block types for the queen-size quilt.

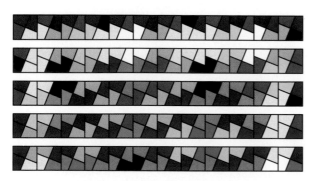

Partial Assembly Diagram

Sew Easy

When you lay out your quilt blocks or pieces, step back often and view the quilt from a distance. Leave the room for awhile, and see if the layout still suits you when you return. Arrange and rearrange the blocks until you are satisfied with the overall design before you stitch them all together.

5	2	2	2	2	2	2	2	2	2	5
2	6	4	3	4	3	4	3	4	3	6	2
2	3	1	1	1	1	1	1	1	1	4	2
2	4	1	1	1	1	1	1	1	1	3	2
2	3	1	1	1	1	1	1	1	1	4	2
2	4	1	1	1	1	1	1	1	1	3	2
2	3	1	1	1	1	1	1	1	1	4	2
2	4	1	1	1	1	1	1	1	1	3	2
2	3	1	1	1	1	1	1	1	1	4	2
2	4	1	1	1	1	1	1	1	1	3	2
2	3	1	1	1	1	1	1	1	1	4	2
2	6	4	3	4	3	4	3	4	3	6	2
5	2	2	2	2	2	2	2	2	2	5

Lap

Diagram 9

5	2	2	2	2	2	2	2	2	2	2	2	2	2	2	2	5
2	6	4	3	4	3	4	3	4	3	4	3	4	3	4	6	2
2	3	1	1	1	1	1	1	1	1	1	1	1	1	1	3	2
2	4	1	1	1	1	1	1	1	1	1	1	1	1	1	4	2
2	3	1	1	1	1	1	1	1	1	1	1	1	1	1	3	2
2	4	1	1	1	1	1	1	1	1	1	1	1	1	1	4	2
2	3	1	1	1	1	1	1	1	1	1	1	1	1	1	3	2
2	4	1	1	1	1	1	1	1	1	1	1	1	1	1	4	2
2	4	1	1	1	1	1	1	1	1	1	1	1	1	1	3	2
2	3	1	1	1	1	1	1	1	1	1	1	1	1	1	4	2
2	3	1	1	1	1	1	1	1	1	1	1	1	1	1	3	2
2	4	1	1	1	1	1	1	1	1	1	1	1	1	1	4	2
2	3	1	1	1	1	1	1	1	1	1	1	1	1	1	3	2
2	4	1	1	1	1	1	1	1	1	1	1	1	1	1	4	2
2	3	1	1	1	1	1	1	1	1	1	1	1	1	1	3	2
2	4	1	1	1	1	1	1	1	1	1	1	1	1	1	4	2
2	3	1	1	1	1	1	1	1	1	1	1	1	1	1	3	2
2	4	1	1	1	1	1	1	1	1	1	1	1	1	1	4	2
2	6	3	4	3	4	3	4	3	4	3	4	3	4	3	6	2
5	2	2	2	2	2	2	2	2	2	2	2	2	2	2	2	5

Queen

Diagram 10

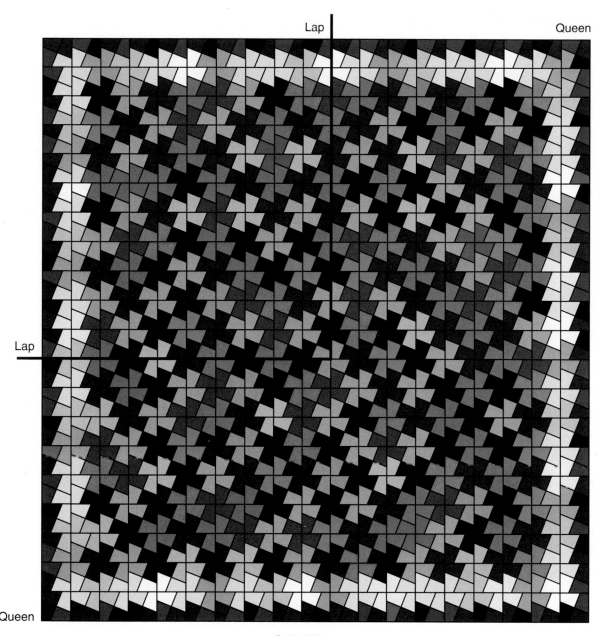

Lap

Queen

Lap

Queen

Quilt Diagram

Step 2. Sew the blocks together into rows. Press the seams in adjoining rows in opposite directions, then sew the rows together, matching seams carefully to complete the quilt top, as shown in the **Quilt Diagram**. Notice that the **Quilt Diagram** shows both the lap quilt and the queen-size quilt. The outline for the lap quilt indicates where the inner pinwheel blocks stop. You will actually have a quilt that is two blocks wider,

as you will need to attach the outer rows of lighter-color border blocks (Blocks 2, 3, and 4), as indicated in **Diagram 9**. Press the quilt top.

QUILTING AND FINISHING

Step 1. Mark the quilt top for quilting. The quilt shown was quilted with gently flowing curves that move across the entire surface of the quilt, made with pattern piece B. Beginning in one corner of the quilt, match the straight lines of B with the seams in each block, as shown in **Diagram 11**. Mark along the curved edge to create continuous wavy lines across the quilt top.

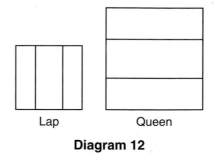

Diagram 12

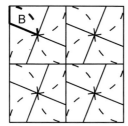

Diagram 11

Step 2. Regardless of which quilt size you've chosen to make, the backing will have to be pieced. For the lap quilt, cut the backing fabric in half crosswise, and trim the selvages. Cut one piece in half lengthwise to make two half-panels. Cut a 29-inch-wide segment from the remaining piece. Sew a half-panel to each side of the 29-inch panel, as shown in **Diagram 12**. Press the seams open.

Step 3. For the queen-size quilt, cut the backing fabric crosswise into three equal lengths, and trim the selvages. Cut a 34-inch-wide panel from two of the pieces. Sew a 34-inch panel to each side of the remaining full-width piece, as shown. Press the seams open.

Step 4. Layer the quilt top, batting, and backing, and baste the layers together. Quilt as desired.

Step 5. Referring to the directions on page 121, make and attach double-fold binding. To calculate the amount of binding needed for the quilt size you are making, add the length of the four sides of the quilt plus 9 inches. The total is the approximate number of inches of binding you will need.

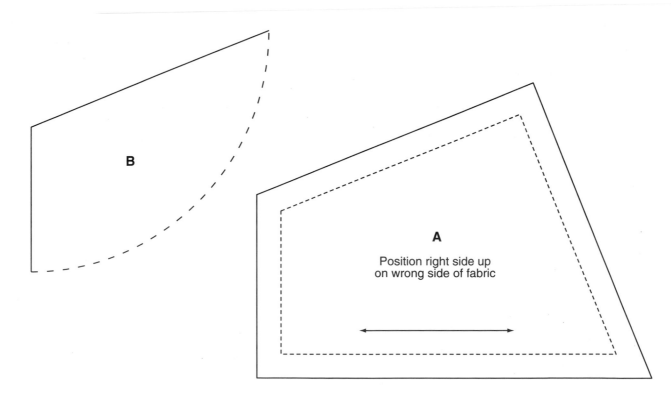

B

A
Position right side up
on wrong side of fabric

NATURAL BALANCE
Color Plan

Photocopy this page and use it to experiment with color schemes for your quilt.

MOUNTAIN MIRAGE

Skill Level: *Challenging*

$\mathbb{K}$athryn Kuhn designed this original twin-size quilt by elongating the traditional One Patch hexagon shape. The blues, purples, teals, and greens she used are reminiscent of a cool evening spent in the mountains, when disappearing daylight casts luminous blue and violet shadows over the range. If you love hand piecing or are up to the challenge of machine piecing numerous set-in seams, you'll enjoy working on this inspirational beauty. Or try the wallhanging version for an appealing addition to your home.

BEFORE YOU BEGIN

Although our instructions are for machine piecing this quilt, it is equally suitable for hand piecing. Either the English paper piecing method or traditional hand sewing would work well for constructing the quilt. For additional information, see "English Paper Piecing" on page 109.

CHOOSING FABRICS

To make a quilt similar to the one shown, choose as many fabrics as possible in a range of color values from light to dark. The quiltmaker chose varying shades of blue, purple, and green for the quilt in the photograph. An assortment of black prints was added to provide both depth and shadow. For more information about working with color value, refer to page 106.

The yardage estimates are just that, and they may be more helpful if you plan to limit the number of fabrics used. As with many other scrappy One Patch

Quilt Sizes		
	Wallhanging	**Twin (shown)**
Finished Quilt Size	37½" × 51"	64½" × 87¾"
Number of Hexagons	401	803

Materials		
	Wallhanging	**Twin**
Assorted light prints	1½ yards	2¾ yards
Assorted medium prints	1⅝ yards	3¼ yards
Assorted dark prints	1⅛ yards	2¼ yards
Black print	1½ yards	2⅛ yards
Backing	2⅝ yards	5⅜ yards
Batting	46" × 59"	73" × 96"
Binding	⅜ yard	¾ yard

NOTE: *Yardages are based on 44/45-inch-wide fabrics that are at least 42 inches wide after preshrinking.*

quilts, the yardage requirements may be best regarded by considering the number of pieces you will use. Refer to the Cutting Chart for the suggested number of hexagons you must cut from each value range. Scraps work wonderfully for this quilt, since each full hexagon can be cut

from leftover pieces of fabric as small as 3 × 4½ inches.

If you like the design of the quilt but would prefer a different color combination, you may want to experiment by photocopying the **Color Plan** on page 17 and using crayons or colored pencils to develop your own personal

Cutting Chart

Fabric	Used For	Piece	Number to Cut Wallhanging	Twin
Light prints	Patchwork	A	141	290
Medium prints	Patchwork	A	160	340
Dark prints	Patchwork	A	100	215
Black print	Edge of patchwork	B	12	22
	Edge of patchwork	C	74	73
	Edge of patchwork	D		1
	Edge of patchwork	D reverse		1
	Border	7" strip	7	9

color scheme. By changing to "hot" colors or perhaps primary colors, the mountains may disappear, but you may be surprised at the exciting new designs that emerge.

CUTTING

Construct durable templates from pattern pieces A, B, C, and D on page 16. For hand piecing, trace and cut your templates on the dashed seam line. For machine piecing, we recommend making a window template so you can cut your fabric on the cutting line and also trace the stitching line on the wrong side of the fabric for easier setting in and pivoting. The patterns also have pivot points marked where the seam lines intersect. Even if you don't trace the whole seam line on the back of your fabric, it is helpful to transfer these pivot points to make assembling the patchwork easier. For more information about making window templates, see page 110.

All measurements include ¼-inch seam allowances. Refer to the Cutting Chart for the number of each piece to cut. The numbers to cut are based on the color values used in the original quilt. If you would like to change the layout of your quilt, lightening or darkening its overall appearance for instance, alter the number of pieces needed from each value. You may find it helpful to cut extra pieces from all colors and values to give

you more design options when laying out the quilt.

Note: Cut and piece together a few samples of each template before cutting all the fabric for the quilt.

— Sew Easy

Sort all of your A pieces by color and value. Reclosable plastic bags make great see-through storage compartments for small pieces such as these. You'll find it much quicker and easier to lay out your quilt top with your pieces categorized and ready to go.

ARRANGING THE QUILT TOP

To make a quilt similar to the original, use a design wall to arrange your hexagons to closely match the colors and values shown in the photograph on page 10. Although you can duplicate the layout fairly easily, this is your quilt, so be creative with your layout and have fun!

Step 1. The A hexagons are arranged in horizontal rows, as shown in **Diagram 1**, with the long sides positioned vertically. The 60 degree tips of hexagons in adjacent rows fit into the pockets created by their upper and lower neighbors. In both the twin-size quilt and the wallhanging, Row 1 contains 36 hexagons. Row 2 contains 37 hexagons and begins to the left of the first row, as shown in **Diagram 1**. Continue to stagger rows in the same manner as you work down the quilt top. The twin-size quilt has a total of 22 rows, while the wallhanging has 11 rows.

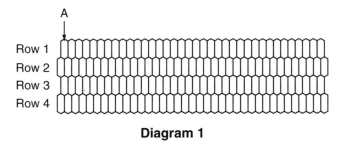

Diagram 1

Step 2. A few basic shapes were used to design the original quilt. Medium to dark pyramids, such as those illustrated in **Diagram 2**, were used to create the images of mountains. Inverted pyramids of varying size, color, and value were used to shade and highlight the mountains. Try arranging your colors in a variety of these large and small pyramids to design your quilt, adding your own variations if you like.

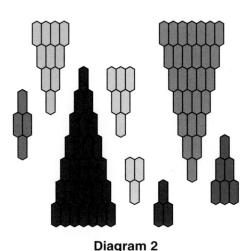

Diagram 2

Step 3. Once you've finished the layout and are satisfied with color placement, place the black B

pieces along the side edges of your quilt, as shown in **Diagram 3**. Place the black C pieces along the top and bottom of your quilt, as shown.

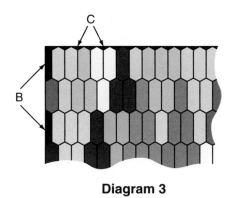

Diagram 3

Step 4. If you're making the twin-size quilt, you'll need one black D and one D reverse piece for the bottom corners, as shown in **Diagram 4**. No D pieces are needed for the wallhanging.

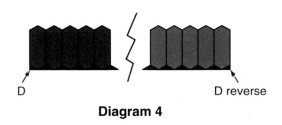

Diagram 4

ASSEMBLING THE QUILT TOP

Throughout the construction of this quilt, the hexagons and triangles will require set-in seams. Refer to page 108 for complete details about setting in seams.

Step 1. For the top row, sew one side of each C triangle to the patch directly to its right, as shown in **Diagram 5** on page 14. Stop sewing at the pivot point (indicated by the dot on the diagram)—the intersection of seam lines you marked on the back of each piece—and backstitch. The bottom row is assembled in the same manner as for the wallhanging. For the twin size, a D triangle is used in the lower left corner and a D reverse triangle is used in the lower right corner.

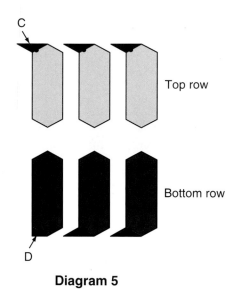

Diagram 5

Step 4. Sew the rows together, pivoting to set in the tips of the hexagons, as shown in **Diagram 8**. Press the quilt.

Diagram 8

Step 2. Sew the pieces in the top row together. Begin sewing at the outermost edge of a C piece, and pivot to set in the seam, as indicated in **Diagram 6**. Stop sewing at the pivot point on the opposite end of the hexagon, since another hexagon will be set into those junctions when the rows are joined, and backstitch. Sew the pieces in the bottom row together in a similar manner.

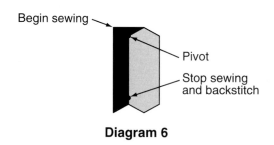

Diagram 6

Step 3. Sew the hexagons and black B pieces in the remaining rows together side by side, beginning and ending each seam at the pivot point, as shown in **Diagram 7**. Remember to backstitch at the beginning and end of each seam.

Diagram 7

ADDING THE MITERED BORDER

The quilt shown has a wide mitered border. See the **Quilt Diagram.** The directions for the wallhanging don't call for a border, as indicated by the lines on the diagram. If you're making the wallhanging, skip to "Quilting and Finishing."

Step 1. To determine the length of the side borders, measure the quilt top vertically through the center. To this measurement, add two times the finished width of the border, plus 5 inches ($6\frac{1}{2}$ inches $\times$ 2 + 5 inches = 18 inches). This is the length you will need to make the two side borders. In the same manner, measure the quilt top horizontally through the center to calculate the length of the top and bottom borders.

Step 2. Sew the 7-inch-wide black border strips together end to end until you've achieved four strips of the lengths you calculated in Step 1.

Step 3. Center, pin, and sew the four borders to the quilt top. Refer to page 119 for instructions on adding borders with mitered corners.

QUILTING AND FINISHING

Step 1. Mark the quilt top for quilting. Each piece in the quilt shown was outline quilted. The hexagon motif was continued in the borders.

Twin | Wallhanging | Twin

Wallhanging

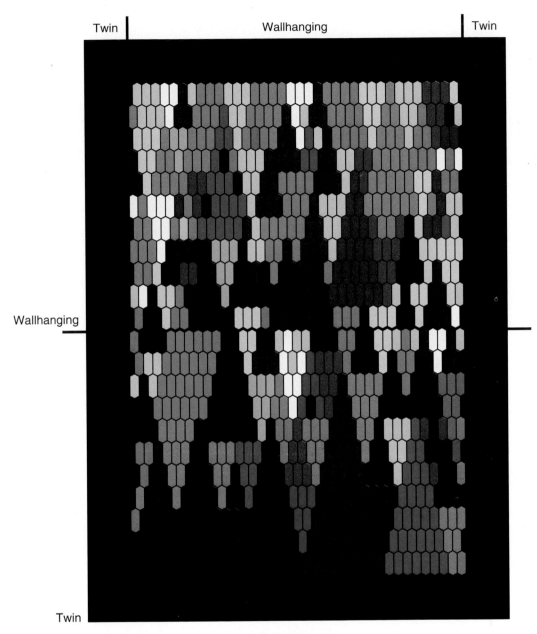

Twin

Quilt Diagram

Step 2. Regardless of which quilt size you've chosen to make, the backing will have to be pieced. For the wallhanging, cut the backing fabric crosswise into two equal pieces, and trim the selvages. Cut one piece in half lengthwise. Cut a 20-inch lengthwise panel from the remaining piece. Sew one of the slightly wider panels to each side of the 20-inch-wide panel, as shown in **Diagram 9.** Press the seams open.

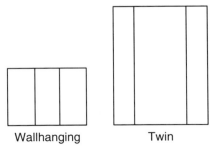

Wallhanging   Twin

Diagram 9

Sew Easy

Since you've already made a durable hexagon template for piecing, you have a ready-made quilting template. Use the same plastic template used for tracing and cutting fabric pieces to trace the hexagon quilting motif on the borders.

Step 3. For the twin-size quilt, cut the backing fabric crosswise into two equal pieces, and trim the selvages. Cut two 17-inch-wide panels lengthwise from one piece. Sew a narrow panel to each side of the full-width piece, as shown in **Diagram 9** on page 15. Press the seams open.

Step 4. Layer the quilt top, batting, and backing, and baste together. Quilt as desired.

Step 5. Referring to page 121, make and attach double-fold binding. To calculate the amount of binding needed for your quilt size, add the length of the four sides of the quilt plus 9 inches. The total is the approximate number of inches of binding you will need.

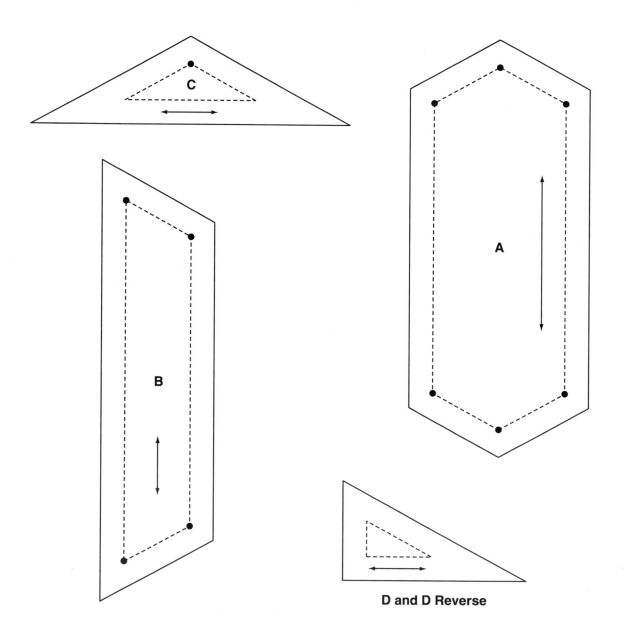

D and D Reverse

MOUNTAIN MIRAGE
Color Plan

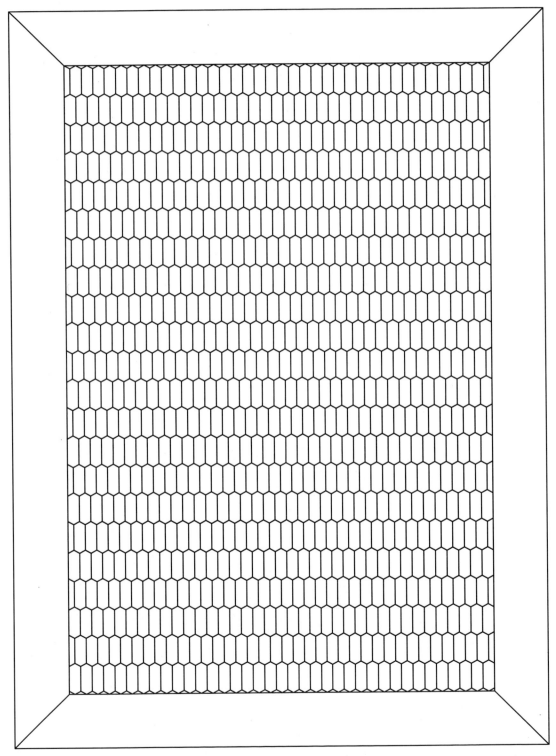

Photocopy this page and use it to experiment with color schemes for your quilt.

6 ÷ 3 = 5

Skill Level: *Intermediate*

*W*hat do you get when you sew three five-sided pieces of fabric together? A hexagon, of course! Edith Zimmer arranged her pieced hexagons in diagonal bands of rainbow colors in this intriguing lap quilt, which would also work well as a wallhanging or crib quilt. Although hexagons have been used to make One Patch quilts for 150 years, this divided hexagon has a decidedly contemporary flair.

BEFORE YOU BEGIN

Three pentagons all cut from the same template but of different color values are sewn together to create a three-dimensional effect in each pieced hexagon in this quilt. The rows of hexagons are then joined in diagonal rows and appliquéd to a preconstructed, pieced border. The quilt shown in the photograph was machine pieced, but it is equally suitable for hand piecing.

CHOOSING FABRICS

The hexagon units in each diagonal row of this quilt are sewn with fabrics from the same color families, but with different color values. A rainbow of colors was used, and colors shift diagonally across the quilt top. For more information about color value, see page 106.

Although some hexagons in the quilt are darker overall than their neighbors, the placement of color value is consistent from unit to unit. The darkest fabric in each unit is always positioned on

Quilt Sizes

	Lap (shown)	Double
Finished Quilt Size	50" × 68"	85" × 108½"
Finished Hexagon Size	4½"	4½"
Number of Hexagons	148	472

Materials

	Lap	Double
Reds	⅓ yard	⅝ yard
Grays	⅓ yard	⅝ yard
Blues	1⅛ yards	3½ yards
Purples	⅓ yard	1⅓ yards
Pinks, roses, and wines	¾ yard	2 yards
Peaches	½ yard	1⅓ yards
Greens	¾ yard	2 yards
Golds, yellows, neutrals, and browns	1⅜ yards	4 yards
Red solid	½ yard	⅞ yard
Navy solid	⅓ yard	¾ yard
Green solid	⅓ yard	¾ yard
Backing	4⅛ yards	8¼ yards
Batting	56" × 71"	94" × 110"
Binding	½ yard	¾ yard

NOTE: *Yardages are based on 44/45-inch-wide fabrics that are at least 42 inches wide after preshrinking.*

Cutting Chart

Fabric	Used For	Piece	Number to Cut Lap	Number to Cut Double
Red and grays				
Light	Patchwork	A	10	20
Medium	Patchwork	A	10	20
Dark	Patchwork	A	10	20
Blues				
Light	Patchwork	A	32	111
Medium	Patchwork	A	32	111
Dark	Patchwork	A	32	111
Purples				
Light	Patchwork	A	10	42
Medium	Patchwork	A	10	42
Dark	Patchwork	A	10	42
Pinks, roses, and wines				
Light	Patchwork	A	22	63
Medium	Patchwork	A	22	63
Dark	Patchwork	A	22	63
Peaches				
Light	Patchwork	A	11	42
Medium	Patchwork	A	11	42
Dark	Patchwork	A	11	42
Greens				
Light	Patchwork	A	22	63
Medium	Patchwork	A	22	63
Dark	Patchwork	A	22	63
Golds, yellows, neutrals, and browns				
Light	Patchwork	A	41	131
Medium	Patchwork	A	41	131
Dark	Patchwork	A	41	131
Red solid	Border	5½" strip	3	5
Navy solid	Border	5½" strip	2	4
Green solid	Border	5½" strip	2	4

the lower left, and the medium fabric is on the lower right. The lightest fabric of the trio is always on top. **Diagram 1** illustrates four typical units.

To make a quilt similar to the one shown, choose an assortment of fabrics from the color families suggested in the Cutting Chart. This quilt is a great way to use scraps, since each pentagon can be cut from a 3 × 4½-inch piece.

For a completely different look, consider a bold color scheme of red, white, black, and a splash of bright yellow. Or perhaps deeper, antique shades of golds, greens, browns, and reds suit your style better. If you would like to create your own color design, the **Color Plan** on page 27 will be helpful. Make photocopies of it, then fill in the spaces with colored pencils or markers until you are satisfied with the design and color placement.

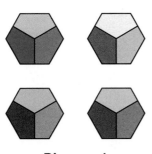

Diagram 1

CUTTING

Construct a durable template of pattern piece A on page 26, since it will be used to cut all of the pieces for the quilt top. For hand piecing, mark the seam line and cutting line. For machine piecing, only the cutting line is necessary, since the dot on the pattern indicates where you will need to pivot to set in your pieces. Transfer the dot to the reverse side of each piece to help improve the accuracy of setting in seams. For more information about constructing templates, see page 116.

All measurements include ¼-inch seam allowances. Refer to the Cutting Chart for the recommended number of A pieces to cut from each color. We suggest you cut a few extra pieces from each color grouping to give more flexibility in arranging pieces and making substitutions when you lay out the quilt.

If you choose to alter the color scheme, you may need different numbers of your colors, but in general, you will need 148 A pieces each of dark, medium, and light fabrics for the lap quilt. For the double quilt, you will need 472 A pieces each of dark, medium, and light fabrics.

Note: Cut and piece a few sample hexagon units before cutting all the fabric for the quilt.

ASSEMBLING THE 3-D HEXAGONS

Step 1. Use a design wall to arrange the individual pentagons into hexagon units before you actually sew anything together. This will allow you to rearrange individual pieces instead of entire hexagon units, giving you more control over the overall look of the quilt. Refer to **Diagram 1** for value placement within each hexagon unit. The **Lap Assembly Diagram** shows diagonal rows within the quilt top to help you position the cut pieces.

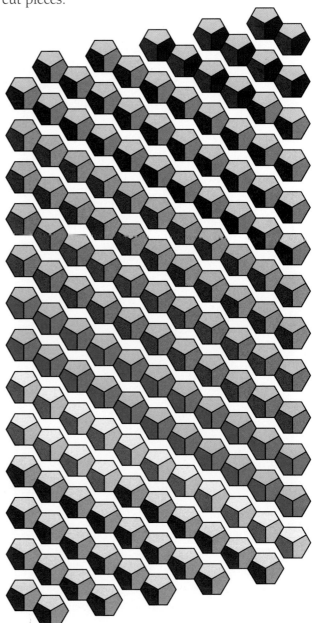

Lap Assembly Diagram

······· Sew **Q**uick ········

For a completely random look, you can piece the pentagons together first into the 3-D hexagons without laying out each individual piece on a design wall. Then to alter your final quilt layout, simply move the pieced hexagons instead of individual pentagons. This method will save layout time, but offers a bit less flexibility in your final color placement.

Stitch to dot, pivot, realign
edges, and stitch to end
Diagram 3

Step 4. Sew the hexagons into diagonal rows, as shown in the **Lap Assembly Diagram** on page 21. Begin and end seams at pivot points (¼ inch from the edge) of each pair so the next row can be set in. Backstitch at the end of seams. See **Diagram 4.**

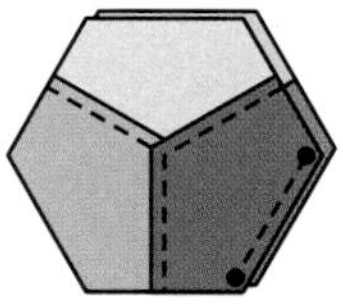

Diagram 4

There are 18 diagonal rows for the lap quilt. For the double quilt, you will have 32 diagonal rows, with the longest rows containing 21 hexagons. Refer also to the **Lap Quilt Diagram** on page 25 and the photograph on page 18 for an overview of the entire quilt top.

Step 2. Once you are satisfied with your color arrangement, sew each group of three pentagons together into hexagon units. Align two pentagons with right sides together, as shown in **Diagram 2.** Begin your seam ¼ inch from the edge of the pieces, at the pivot point, as shown, backstitching at the beginning of the seam.

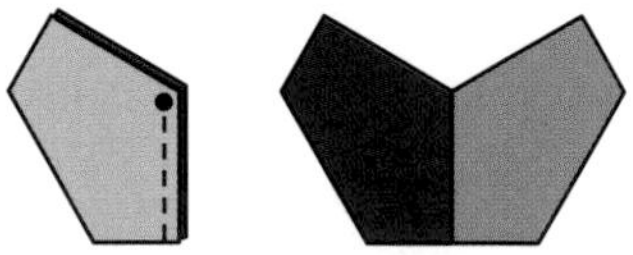

Step 5. Sew the diagonal rows together, pivoting and setting in seams where the corners of hexagons meet, as shown in **Diagram 5.** Begin and end each seam at a pivot point, and backstitch at each end. Press seams to lie flat.

Start sewing
at dot,
backstitch,
and stitch
to end

Open pieces
and press

Diagram 2

Step 3. Sew the third pentagon to the unit, pivoting and setting in the seam, as indicated in **Diagram 3.** See page 108 for more information about setting in seams. Press seams so they lie flat. Repeat to complete the number of hexagon units required for your quilt size.

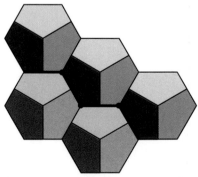

Stitch rows together, pivoting at dots
Diagram 5

Step 6. Turn under the ¼-inch seam allowance of all outer hexagons. Baste the edges in place so they can easily be appliquéd to the border.

Sew Easy

A pressing template can simplify the task of turning under edges. Use a heat-resistant template material, available at most quilt shops, to construct a *finished size* template of the complete *hexagon* unit. Working from the wrong side of the quilt, fit the template snugly against the stitched seams of an outer hexagon, then press the outer seam allowance over the template. A bit of spray starch collected in a small container can be applied with a cotton swab or small brush to help produce a crisp edge that will stay in place.

ADDING THE BORDER

The completed quilt top is centered on a pre-assembled, pieced border, then appliquéd in place. The border in the quilt in the photo on page 18 was sewn from solid red, navy, and green fabrics. Color shifts were carefully planned, with each change beginning at the outer point of a hexagon unit. Where the colors are joined, the angle of the seam is a continuation of the 60 degree angle of the hexagon side, as shown in the **Lap Quilt Diagram** on page 25. Notice that the four corners of the borders are mitered with 45 degree angles.

Step 1. The top and bottom borders are each cut from one fabric. Measure the width of the quilt top, taking the measurement horizontally through the center of the quilt. Be sure to measure from the outermost points of hexagons. Add 5 inches to this measurement for mitering. Cut or piece one red and one blue border to this length.

Step 2. Each side border is pieced from the three different solid fabrics. First, determine your color scheme and where the color breaks will occur. Calculate the length each strip must be

based on its beginning and ending points in the border, then add several inches to those lengths to allow for cutting 60 degree angles. The extra inches will also give you more flexibility in laying out the border.

Step 3. Lay your quilt on the floor or another flat surface. Place the top and bottom borders under the edges of the quilt top, centering the borders horizontally and extending 2½ inches of each border beyond the top or bottom edge of the quilt. Position the side border strips under the quilt in the same manner, overlapping edges where color breaks will occur by at least 4½ inches. See **Diagram 6.**

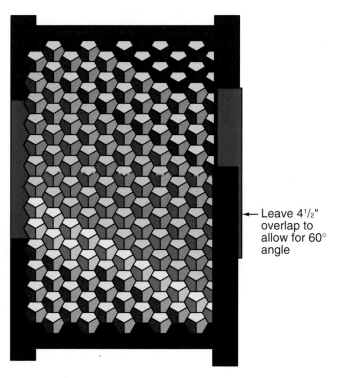

← Leave 4½" overlap to allow for 60° angle

Diagram 6

Step 4. Pin the quilt top to the borders to prevent shifting. Use your rotary ruler to mark a 60 degree line across the border, beginning where you would like the colors to change. Unpin the quilt top from the border, add a ¼-inch seam allowance to the strip, and cut. See **Diagram 7** on page 24. Mark the beginning point of the underneath strip in the same manner, then add a ¼-inch seam allowance in the opposite direction of the allowance you added for the first strip. Pin the borders securely to hold them in place while you finish the remaining color shifts.

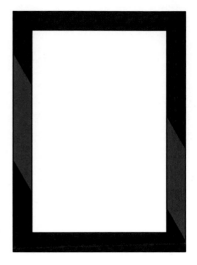

Diagram 8

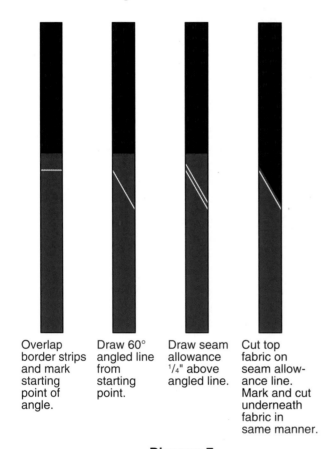

Overlap border strips and mark starting point of angle.

Draw 60° angled line from starting point.

Draw seam allowance ¼" above angled line.

Cut top fabric on seam allowance line. Mark and cut underneath fabric in same manner.

Diagram 7

Step 5. When the color shifts in the side borders have all been marked and cut, sew the segments together. Press seams. Position the borders along the quilt sides, then mark the corner miters where the side borders intersect the top and bottom borders. For more information on preparing miters, see page 119. Unpin the borders from the quilt top and sew the side borders to the top and bottom borders with a ¼-inch seam allowance. See **Diagram 8**. Press seams.

Step 6. Reposition the quilt on top of the borders. Pin to hold it in place, then baste around all edges. Machine or hand appliqué the quilt top to the border around the outer edges of the hexagons.

----- Sew **Q**uick -----

To make a border from a single fabric, determine the lengths required for all sides of the quilt top. Measure the quilt top vertically through its center and add 4½ inches. This is the length required for each side border. Measure the quilt top horizontally through its center and subtract 10 inches. This is the length required for both the top and bottom border. Since the quilt top is staggered, be sure both measurements reflect the distance between outermost hexagons. Sew the 5½-inch-wide border strips together to achieve the calculated lengths. Sew the completed border strips together, as shown, to make a frame for the quilt top.

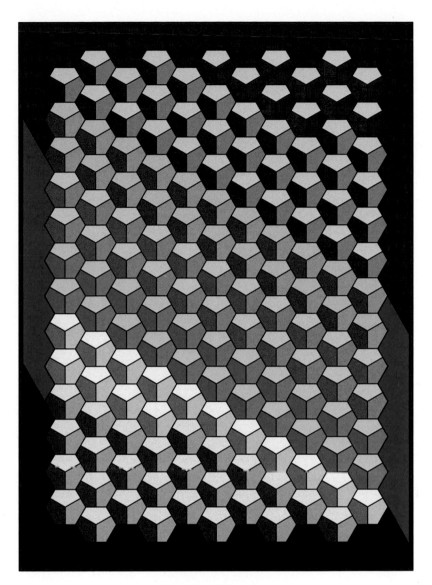

Lap Quilt Diagram

QUILTING AND FINISHING

Step 1. Mark the quilt top for quilting. In the quilt shown, diagonal lines were quilted in both directions through the centers of the hexagons. The hexagons along the edges were outline quilted.

Step 2. Regardless of which quilt size you've chosen to make, the backing will have to be pieced. **Diagram 9** illustrates the two quilt backs. For the lap quilt, cut the backing fabric in half crosswise, and trim the selvages. Cut two 10-inch-wide pieces lengthwise from one of the segments, then sew one of the narrow segments to each side of the full-width piece, as shown. Press seams open.

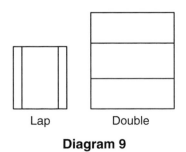

Lap   Double

Diagram 9

Step 3. For the double quilt, cut the backing fabric crosswise into three equal-length pieces, and trim the selvages. Cut a 36-inch-wide panel from two of the pieces. Sew a narrow panel to each side of the full-width panel, as shown in **Diagram 9** on page 25. Press seams open.

Step 4. Layer the quilt top, batting, and backing, and baste the layers together. Quilt as desired.

Step 5. Referring to the directions on page 121, make and attach double-fold binding. To calculate the amount of binding needed for your quilt, add the length of the four sides of the quilt plus 9 inches. The total is the approximate number of inches of binding you will need. The quilt shown has two colors of binding—red and blue. To do

the same, calculate the amount of binding needed for each color, adding 9 inches to each amount to allow for overlaps. Begin sewing the binding to the quilt as directed on page 121. When you near the spot where you want the first color to end, cut away the excess tail of binding, but leave enough binding to extend slightly past the point where the color shift will take place.

Fold under the raw edge of the second color, and sew the binding to the quilt in the usual manner, beginning at the exact spot where colors change. Backstitch at the beginning of the seam.

Repeat the same procedure for each color shift in the binding.

Before sewing the binding to the back of the quilt, blindstitch the overlapped, folded edges at color shifts to the binding fabric below.

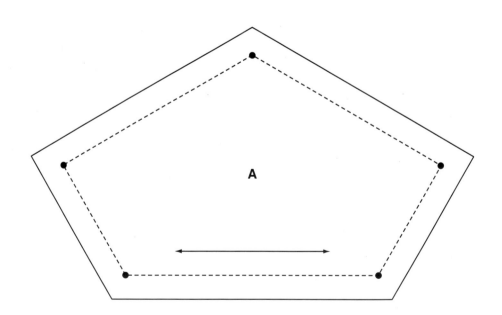

6 ÷ 3 = 5

Color Plan

Photocopy this page and use it to experiment with color schemes for your quilt.

GRANDMOTHER'S FLOWER GARDEN

Skill Level: *Intermediate*

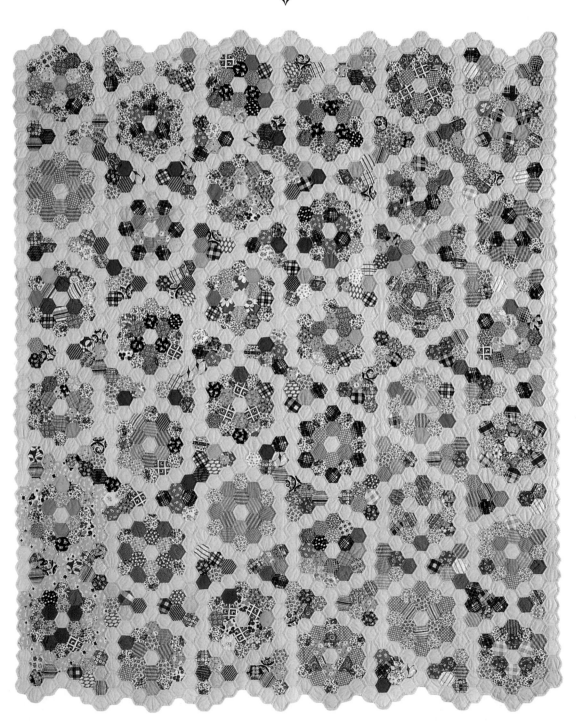

*W*hat collection of One Patch quilts would be complete without a sparkling example of a Grandmother's Flower Garden? This cheerful yellow quilt was pieced in the late 1930s by Lelia Poindexter, who used a delightful assortment of whimsical prints typical of that era. For 60 years, the quilt top waited patiently until it was given to Lelia's great-granddaughter, Kathryn Jones, in 1994. Kathryn moved some of the flower units from the side of the quilt to the bottom to make it a traditional twin size before quilting and binding it.

BEFORE YOU BEGIN

The quilt in the photograph was hand pieced, and the directions that follow are also for hand piecing using the English paper piecing method. For this method, you will need to cut paper hexagons as well as fabric hexagons using pattern piece A on page 34. If you prefer to machine piece, refer to page 108 for information about setting in seams.

CHOOSING FABRICS

This scrap quilt is assembled with solid yellow hexagons and hexagons cut mostly from prints of a medium color value. For a scrap quilt such as this, variety is important, so try to choose as many fabrics as possible for your medium hexagons. For an explanation of color value, see page 106.

While the overall look of this quilt is scrappy, the background fabric is also an important feature, made even more prominent when it's such a bold sunshine

yellow. Photocopy the **Color Plan** on page 35, and use crayons or colored pencils to experiment with other background colors, such as soft green, blue, or off-white. You can also use the **Color Plan** to try different color arrangements within the flowers.

CUTTING

Pattern piece A includes ¼-inch seam allowances. Refer to the Cutting Chart on page 30 for the types and number of A pieces you must cut. We suggest you make a window template of piece A, which will enable you to mark

Quilt Sizes		
	Wallhanging	**Twin (shown)**
Finished Quilt Size	41¼" × 46¼"	78¾" × 97"
Number of Flower Units	7	36
Number of Six-Hexagon Clusters	10	60
Number of Three-Hexagon Clusters	2	12

Materials		
	Wallhanging	**Twin**
Yellow	1 yard	4¾ yards
Medium prints	1⅜ yards	6⅜ yards
Backing	1⅝ yards	5⅝ yards
Batting	50" × 55"	87" × 105"
Bias binding	15" square	24" square
Paper for piecing		

NOTE: Yardages are based on 44/45-inch-wide fabrics that are at least 42 inches wide after preshrinking.

29

Cutting Chart

Fabric	Used For	Piece	Number to Cut	
			Wallhanging	Twin
Yellow	Background and flower centers	A	147	770
Medium prints	Flowers and clusters	A	205	1,044
Paper	English paper piecing	A	220	1,130

NOTE: *Fabric hexagons are cut on outer, solid lines; paper hexagons are cut on inner, dashed lines.*

both the cutting line and seam line with the same template. A window template also makes it easy to target and center specific areas of a print within a hexagon, as shown in **Diagram 1.** For more information about window templates, see page 110.

Diagram 1

Fabric hexagons are cut on the outside line of the template. Mark and cut paper pieces to the finished size of the hexagon (the inside line). Paper pieces can be reused, so you won't need one for each fabric piece in the quilt unless you choose to leave all papers in place until the quilt top is complete.

Many types of paper can be used. Card stock–weight paper works well, but some quilters prefer ordinary typing paper. Freezer paper is another option and eliminates the need for seam basting. Precut paper pieces are also available and can be purchased in a variety of sizes. For this quilt, you would need to purchase paper hexagons that are 1¼ inches on each side.

Note: Cut and piece one sample flower unit before cutting all the fabric for the quilt.

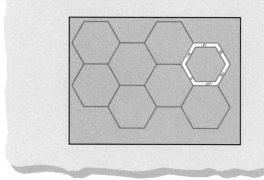

To minimize waste of fabric or paper and to shorten your cutting time by half, mark both your fabric and paper hexagons as shown here, with no space between adjacent hexagons. By aligning the sides of all hexagons, a single cut does the job for two different hexagons.

MAKING THE HEXAGON UNITS

Three types of hexagon units are used in this quilt: flower units that contain both medium print and yellow solid hexagons, six-hexagon clusters of medium print fabric, and three-hexagon clusters of medium print fabric. The units are assembled individually, then sewn together in diagonal rows. The rows are then joined, and additional hexagons are sewn around the outer perimeter of the quilt to complete the quilt top.

Flower Units

Each flower unit has a yellow hexagon at its center and is surrounded by two rows of medium print hexagons. An outer ring of yellow hexagons completes the unit. See **Diagram 2.** You will need 19 yellow and 18 print hexagons for each flower.

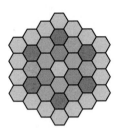

Diagram 2

Step 1. Center a paper hexagon on the wrong side of a yellow fabric hexagon and pin it in place. Fold the seam allowance over the paper piece, one side at a time, and press in place. Baste the seam allowances to the paper hexagon, making sure they are secure where each folded edge meets. See **Diagram 3.** Repeat with all remaining yellow and print hexagons needed for one flower unit.

If you are using freezer paper, position a paper hexagon on the reverse side of a fabric hexagon, with the waxy side of the paper facing up. Use a medium-hot dry iron to press the seam allowances onto the paper.

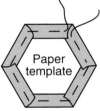

Diagram 3

Step 2. Place a yellow and print hexagon with right sides together, taking care to match all corners of the two pieces exactly. Whipstitch two edges together from corner to corner along one side, backstitching at the beginning and end of the seam. Take small stitches and avoid sewing into the edges of the paper. Your stitches should barely show when the pieces are opened. See **Diagram 4.**

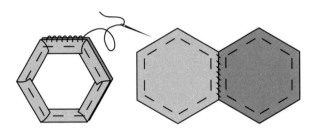

Diagram 4

Step 3. Continue adding print hexagons to the yellow center hexagon, one at a time, matching edges and whipstitching in the same manner as before. After sewing one edge of the print hexagon to the center hexagon, backstitch, then continue sewing its adjacent side to the first hexagon added to the center one, as shown in **Diagram 5.** Don't knot and clip your thread each time you reach the end of a hexagon side. Just backstitch, then reposition the hexagon along the next side to be joined and keep sewing. Backstitch at the end of each seam. Continue adding the remaining print hexagons around the yellow center until the partially assembled flower unit looks like the one in **Diagram 6** on page 32.

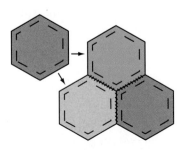

Diagram 5

Diagram 6

Step 4. Sew a second ring of 12 print hexagons around the unit, as shown in **Diagram 7**. Finish the flower by sewing the remaining 18 yellow hexagons around the outer edge. Your flower unit should now resemble **Diagram 2** on page 31.

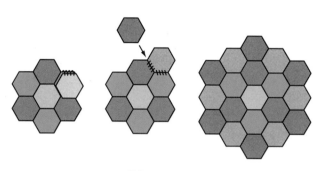

Diagram 7

Step 5. Remove the papers from the inner rings of hexagons carefully so they can be reused. Leave the papers in the outer yellow hexagons in place. Freezer paper templates should not be removed until all edges of one hexagon are sewn to another.

Step 6. Repeat Steps 1 through 5 to assemble the number of flower units required for your quilt size.

Six-Hexagon Units

Baste paper hexagons to six print hexagons in the same manner as for the flower units. Sew the cluster together, as shown in **Diagram 8**. Do not remove the papers. Repeat until you've assembled the required number of six-hexagon units for your quilt size.

Three-Hexagon Units

Prepare three print hexagons as for the flower and six-hexagon units. Sew the hexagons together, as shown in **Diagram 9**. Repeat until you've as-

sembled the required number of three-hexagon units for your quilt size.

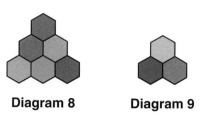

Diagram 8   **Diagram 9**

ASSEMBLING THE QUILT TOP

Step 1. Use a design wall or other flat surface to arrange the quilt's components into diagonal rows, as shown in the assembly diagrams. The top row of the **Wallhanging Assembly Diagram** and the top two rows of the **Twin-Size Assembly Diagram** show the individual hexagon units in each row. The remaining rows are illustrated with their units joined.

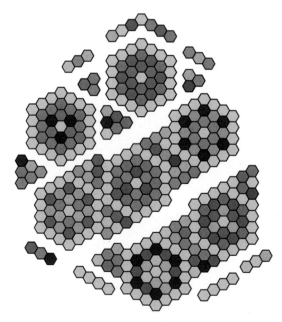

Wallhanging Assembly Diagram

Step 2. Sew the pieces in each diagonal row together, matching all sides of adjoining hexagons and whipstitching them together as before.

Step 3. Sew the completed rows together in the same manner. Finish the top by sewing the re-

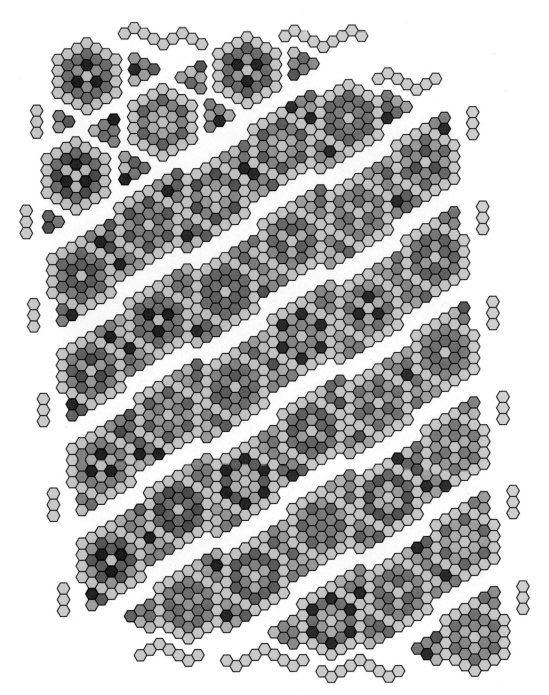

Twin-Size Assembly Diagram

maining yellow hexagons around the outer edge of the twin-size quilt, as indicated in the **Twin-Size Assembly Diagram.** A yellow border of hexagons surrounds the quilt. Gaps in the outer edge of the wallhanging are filled in with yellow and print hexagons. See the **Wallhanging Diagram** on page 34. Refer to both assembly diagrams for placement.

QUILTING AND FINISHING

Step 1. Mark the quilt top for quilting, if desired. Each hexagon in the quilt shown was outline quilted ¼ inch from the seams.

Step 2. Since the wallhanging is less than 42 inches wide, the backing can be cut from a

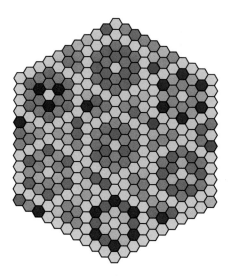

Wallhanging Diagram

through all layers, then trim away excess batting and backing. This step will make adding binding around the many angles on the quilt edges a bit easier.

Or if you prefer to finish your quilt without binding, see page 111 for an alternate edge-finishing method.

single piece of fabric. Press the fabric before using it, and trim the selvages.

Step 3. For the twin-size quilt, cut the backing fabric in half crosswise, and trim the selvages. Cut one piece in half lengthwise. Sew one of the narrow panels to each side of the full-width piece, as shown in **Diagram 10**. Press the seams open.

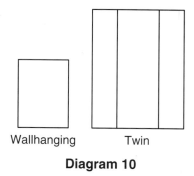

Wallhanging   Twin

Diagram 10

Step 4. Layer the quilt top, batting, and backing, and baste the layers together. Quilt as desired.

Step 5. Referring to the page 110, make and attach single-fold binding, mitering around the corners of each hexagon. You will need approximately 210 inches of binding for the wallhanging and 525 inches of binding for the twin-size quilt. Before attaching the binding, make sure outer edges of the quilt are basted or pinned securely

···········Sew Quick··········

Many quilt and fabric shops sell ¼-inch-wide masking tape for quilters. This product comes in handy for marking the ¼-inch distance from the seam lines for outline quilting. Simply tear off a piece of tape and lay one edge along the seam line. Quilt along the other edge for a perfectly even stitching line. When you have finished quilting along one side of the hexagon, lift the tape, move it to the next edge, and continue quilting. You can reuse a piece of tape several times before needing a new one. Remove the tape as you go to avoid leaving any sticky residue on your quilt top.

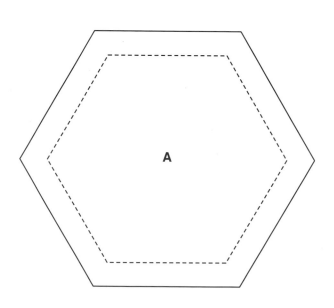

A

GRANDMOTHER'S FLOWER GARDEN

Color Plan

Photocopy this page and use it to experiment with color schemes for your quilt.

Damon's Diamond Delight

Skill Level: *Advanced*

*C*herry Schorfheide began hand piecing a traditional Tumbling Blocks quilt for her son Damon as a way to play with dark, medium, and light fabric scraps. By the time she had pieced all of the individual cubes, she decided her quilt should do more than just tumble. After several days of rearranging, she settled on a magnificent center diamond motif. Cherry certainly achieved her goal—this lap quilt is quite a dazzler!

BEFORE YOU BEGIN

The directions are for hand piecing this quilt using English paper piecing. If you prefer to machine piece, see page 108 for information on sewing set-in seams.

CHOOSING FABRICS

This scrap quilt contains a large assortment of fabrics in three basic color values: light, medium, and dark. For information on color value, see page 106.

The majority of the prints used in this quilt are small, keeping in scale with the 1¼-inch diamond. However, a variety of prints, including florals, stripes, and plaids, were used. A few pieces were cut from fabrics with larger prints.

Probably the most important fabric consideration is that of the border fabrics. The inner and outer borders are cut from a striped fabric designed especially for borders. Stripes, plaids, or other obvious directional prints can also be used. The amount of yardage required will depend on the fabric you choose and how many repeating panels it contains. The strip lengths given in

Quilt Size	
Finished Quilt Size	57¼" × 75½"
Finished Diamond Size	1¼"

NOTE: *Due to the complexity of the design, no size variations are provided.*

Materials	
	Amount
Assorted light prints	1¾ yards
Assorted medium prints	1⅞ yards
Assorted dark prints	1⅞ yards
Green print	1 yard
Border stripe	2¾ yards
Backing	4¾ yards
Batting	66" × 84"
Binding	⅝ yard
Paper for piecing	

NOTE: *Yardages are based on 44/45-inch-wide fabrics that are at least 42 inches wide after preshrinking.*

the Cutting Chart on page 38 are estimates, based on the size of the quilt shown, and are given to help you estimate yardage.

When selecting border fabrics, look for prints with patterns that repeat at short intervals. The mitered corners will be more attractive if the print meets in the

same way at each corner, a trick that is easier to accomplish with a print that repeats every 2 inches rather than every 4 or 5 inches.

CUTTING

Construct durable templates from pattern pieces A, B, and C

Cutting Chart

Fabric	Used For	Piece	Number to Cut
Light prints	Patchwork	A	526
	Patchwork	C	34
Medium prints	Patchwork	A	548
	Patchwork	B	16
	Patchwork	C	21
Dark prints	Patchwork	A	548
	Patchwork	B	16
	Patchwork	C	17
Paper	Hand piecing	A	1,622
	Hand piecing	B	32
	Hand piecing	C	72
Green print	Middle border	4" strips	9
Border stripe	Inner border		See note
	Outer border		See note

NOTE: *Do not cut striped border strips until your quilt top is assembled. Specific cutting information is given in "Cutting," beginning on page 37.*

on page 42, as they will be used to cut hundreds of pieces, and each piece needs to be cut accurately. We suggest you make window templates, which will allow you to mark both the cutting and seam line with the same template. For more information about window templates, see page 110.

Fabric pieces are cut out around the outer, solid line of the template. If you'd like, mark the seam line on the back side of each fabric piece to help you center the finished-size paper pieces.

Paper pieces are marked and cut to the finished size of the template, represented by the inner, dashed line. For information about the English paper piecing technique, see page 109.

All measurements include ¼-inch seam allowances. Refer to the Cutting Chart for the types and number of pieces to cut from each template.

In the quilt shown, the inner border strips were cut 2 inches wide and the outer borders were cut 4¼ inches wide. The strips were cut *lengthwise* to take advantage of the stripe. For the quilt shown, you will need two 72-inch-long inner borders and two 72-inch-long outer borders for the top and bottom of the quilt. For the side borders, you will need four 90-inch-long strips—two for the inner border and two for the outer border. These border lengths allow extra inches for matching patterns and mitering the corners.

If your border fabric has wider or narrower stripes, you will need to adjust the strip width you cut accordingly. This may also affect the overall size of your quilt and the size requirement for the batting and backing fabric.

Note: Cut and assemble one sample piecing unit before cutting all the fabric for the quilt.

MAKING THE CUBE UNITS

You will likely rearrange this quilt's components many times before you are satisfied with the overall design. To give you more options for the quilt's layout, the directions are for assembling small, 3-diamond cubes rather than the 12-diamond unit often used for Tumbling Blocks quilts. The smaller cubes are sewn into rows, then the rows are joined to complete the quilt top.

Step 1. Choose one light, one medium, and one dark fabric A diamond, and cut ⅜ inch off their long tips. Center a paper diamond on the wrong side of each fabric diamond, pin, and fold the fabric tips to meet the tip of the paper, as shown in **Diagram 1A.** Working clockwise, fold the seam allowance over the paper one side at a time and press in place. See **1B.** Baste the seam allowance to the paper, securing the thread ends. See **1C.** Remove the pin. Repeat with the two remaining diamonds.

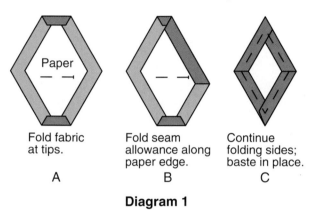

Fold fabric at tips.	Fold seam allowance along paper edge.	Continue folding sides; baste in place.
A	B	C

Diagram 1

Step 2. Referring to **Diagram 2**, align the light and medium diamonds with right sides together. Whipstitch the edges, sewing from corner to corner and backstitching at each end of the seam. Take small stitches so that they barely show when the pieces are opened. Avoid sewing into the paper.

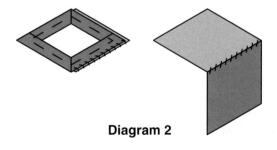

Diagram 2

Step 3. Align the dark and medium diamonds with right sides together, as shown in **Diagram 3A.** Whipstitch the edges together, starting at the outside edge and sewing to the inner corner. Be sure to backstitch at the beginning of the seam. When you reach the end of the seam, backstitch again, but do not cut the thread. Reposition the dark piece so its upper edge is aligned with the

········ Sew **Quick** ········

If you prefer machine piecing, see the Tumbling Blocks quilt on page 94. For that quilt, individual diamonds are arranged on a design wall, then machine sewn into larger units when the layout is complete.

light diamond, as shown in **3B.** Fold the light diamond toward you, so its right side is facing the right side of the dark diamond. Continue stitching. Backstitch at the edge of the seam. Do not remove the papers. Repeat to assemble 525 cube units.

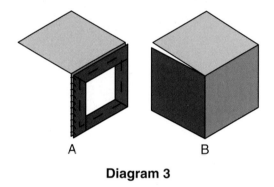

A	B

Diagram 3

ASSEMBLING THE QUILT TOP

Step 1. Lay out the quilt top, as shown in the **Assembly Diagram** on page 40. The large center diamond and four corner sections are pieced from the 525 pieced cubes. To finish the top, side, and bottom edges, you will need A, B, and C pieces, as shown. Color placement is key to this quilt design, so take a look at the following pointers when laying out your quilt:

• Cubes forming the central diamond motif are arranged with the *lightest* diamonds on the top.

• Cubes to the right of the diamond have the *darkest* pieces on the top.

• Cubes to the left of the diamond have *medium* pieces on the top.

• Pieces on the quilt's outer edges that are connected to another piece should be sewn together before being added to the quilt edges.

Assembly Diagram

Step 2. Use the same piecing method to sew the center diamond cubes together in rows, as shown in **Diagram 4,** backstitching at each end of each seam. Do not remove the papers.

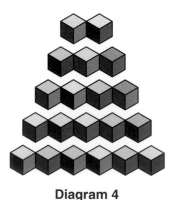

Diagram 4

Step 3. Sew the cubes in each of the four corners together, backstitching at the beginning and end of each seam. Leave the papers in place.

Step 4. Sew the four corners to the center diamond, being careful to have the light, medium, and dark diamonds facing in the right direction. Match adjoining edges as before, and backstitch occasionally to add strength to your seam. Papers may be removed from a piece after all pieces bordering it are sewn in place.

Step 5. Sew each side B triangle to an A diamond, referring to the **Assembly Diagram** for color placement. Then add the units to the sides of the quilt. Finally, sew the C triangles together in pairs, then attach them in the same manner.

Step 6. To complete the bottom of the quilt, first sew a dark C triangle to the left side of the bottom of the large center diamond and a medium C triangle to the right of the large center diamond. Then sew pairs of C triangles to the remaining medium and dark A diamonds, referring to the **Assembly Diagram.** Attach these units to the left and right sides of the bottom of the quilt, referring again to the **Assembly Diagram.**

ADDING THE MITERED BORDERS

Step 1. To determine the correct length for the side borders, measure the quilt top vertically through the center. To this measurement, add two times the finished width of the border, plus 15 inches. (The additional length will help you match the border stripe print at the mitered seams.) This is the length you will need to cut the side borders. In the same manner, measure the quilt top horizontally through the center to calculate the length for the top and bottom borders. Cut the four inner border strips and four outer border strips to your calculated lengths.

Step 2. For the middle border, subtract 10 inches from each measurement calculated in Step 1, and sew the 4-inch-wide green print strips together end to end to assemble four strips of the adjusted lengths. If your inner and outer borders are from a solid or small-print fabric rather than from a border fabric, they can be cut and assembled in this same manner.

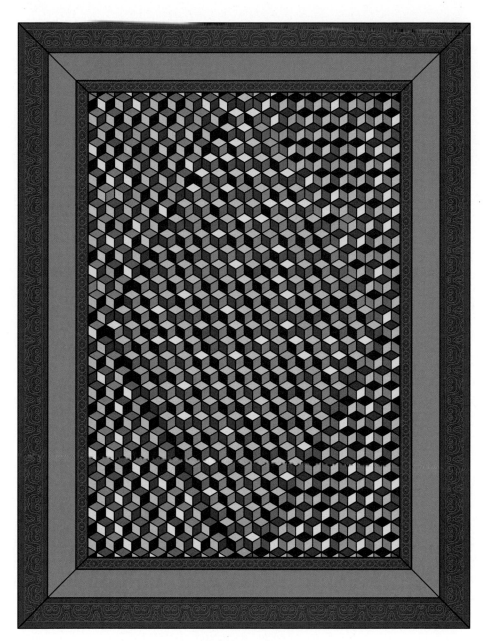

Quilt Diagram

Step 3. Mark the center of each side of the quilt, then lay the quilt on a flat surface. Center the inner side border strips along the sides of the quilt. Carefully position the remaining inner border strips along the top and bottom of the quilt. For a preview of the mitered corner, fold back the border strips at a 45 degree angle where they meet. Shift the top and bottom borders sideways until the design is pleasing. Shift the side borders, too, if necessary. When you have determined the correct strip placement, mark the new center point of each inner border strip so that it can be realigned to the center of the quilt later. See **Diagram 5** on page 42.

Step 4. Center each middle border strip lengthwise on its corresponding inner border, and sew the pairs together with a ¼-inch seam allowance. Press the seams in the side borders toward the middle border. Press the seams in the top and bottom borders in the opposite direction.

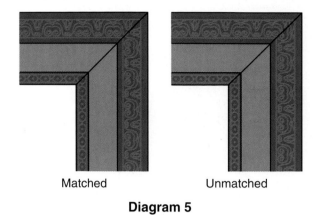

Matched   Unmatched

Diagram 5

Step 5. Place the four border units against the quilt again, matching the marked center of each inner border strip with the center mark on each side of the quilt. Center the outer side border strips along the outer edges of the sewn border units. Position the top and bottom outer borders along the top and bottom sewn units, and shift strips as you did with the inner border to achieve a pleasing design. Sew the outer borders to the partially assembled units, taking care to retain their positions. Press the new seams in the same direction as others in each unit.

Step 6. Pin and sew the four border units to the quilt top, realigning the center points marked on the quilt top with the marks on the inner borders. Refer to page 119 for instructions on adding borders with mitered corners. When preparing the miters, be sure to match like strips in adjacent borders, as shown in the **Quilt Diagram** on page 41.

QUILTING AND FINISHING

Step 1. Mark the quilt top for quilting. Each diamond in the quilt shown was outline quilted. A feather motif was used in the middle border, while straight stitching in the inner and outer borders highlights the designs of the border print.

Step 2. To make the backing, cut the backing fabric in half crosswise, and trim the selvages. Cut two 14-inch-wide segments lengthwise from one piece, then sew a 14-inch panel to each side of the full-width piece, as shown in **Diagram 6.**

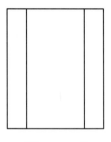

Diagram 6

Step 3. Layer the backing, batting, and quilt top, and baste the layers together. Quilt all marked designs and add any additional quilting as desired.

Step 4. Referring to the directions on page 121, make and attach double-fold binding. To calculate the amount of binding needed, add the length of the four sides of the quilt plus 9 inches. The total is the approximate number of inches of binding you will need.

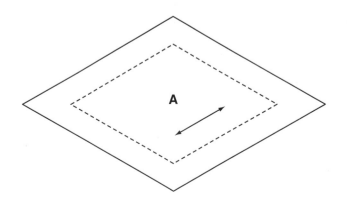

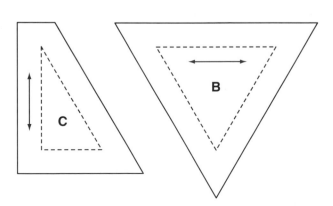

Damon's Diamond Delight
Color Plan

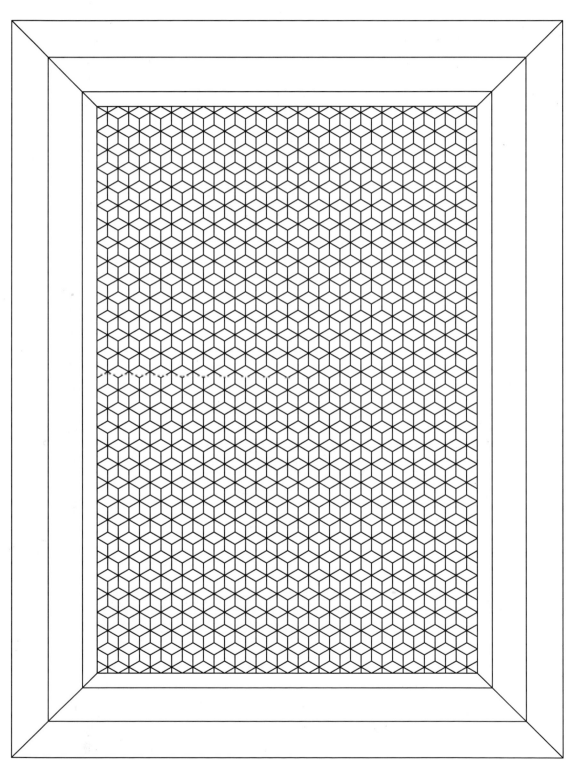

Photocopy this page and use it to experiment with color schemes for your quilt.

Barn Raising Pinwheels

Skill Level: *Easy*

asy enough for a confident beginner, this dynamic double-size quilt offers a bold design that looks harder to piece than it actually is. Pinwheel blocks with dark and light centers are arranged in a barn raising–style setting to create lots of movement, so the viewer's eyes can't help but travel about the quilt top examining the many scraps of fabric. Quiltmaker Barbara Berliner obviously has a sense of humor, having included fabrics with cartoon characters, sneakers, and a guitar along with more traditional florals and prints.

BEFORE YOU BEGIN

The blocks in this machine-pieced quilt go together quickly. At first glance, the design appears complex due to the jagged barn raising setting, but just two block variations are used in the quilt. Blocks have only straight seams, and no setting in is required. The completed blocks are simply rotated to achieve the medallion-style effect.

CHOOSING FABRICS

In the quilt shown, a light gray print and a black print were used for the rows of diagonal pinwheels. These neutral fabrics are surrounded by scraps of vibrant medium to medium-dark fabrics. The scrap fabrics range from bright florals and batiks to juvenile prints (there's even one containing Fred Flintstone!). This quilt would work equally well featuring any two contrasting fabrics for the pinwheels, such as red and white or forest green and tan, with scraps that are as bold or subdued as you like. The most critical design element is that the color value of the scraps be medium to dark. For more information about color value, refer to page 106.

To create your own color scheme for this quilt, photocopy the **Color Plan** on page 51, and use colored pencils, crayons, or markers to fill in the blocks until you are satisfied with the design.

Quilt Sizes		
	Double (shown)	**King**
Finished Quilt Size	80½" × 104½"	104½" × 104½"
Number of Blocks	48	64
Finished Block Size	12"	12"

Materials		
	Double	**King**
Black print	2⅜ yards	3⅛ yards
Light gray print	2⅜ yards	3⅛ yards
Assorted medium prints	4⅝ yards	6⅛ yards
Dark blue	½ yard	⅝ yard
Black	1⅛ yards	1⅛ yards
Backing	7⅝ yards	9⅝ yards
Batting	89" × 113"	113" × 113"
Binding	¾ yard	⅞ yard

NOTE: Yardages are based on 44/45-inch-wide fabrics that are at least 42 inches wide after preshrinking.

45

Cutting Chart

Fabric	Used For	Strip Width	Number to Cut Double	Number to Cut King	Second Cut Piece	Number to Cut Double	Number to Cut King
Black print	Pinwheels	3½"	20	26	A	192	256
Light gray print	Pinwheels	3½"	20	26	A	192	256
Medium prints	Pinwheels	3½"	40	52	A	384	512
Dark blue	Inner border	1½"	10	11			
Black	Outer border	3½"	10	11			

CUTTING

Make a durable template from pattern piece A on page 50—one that will hold up as you cut all the pieces for your quilt from it. For more information about making and using templates, see page 116.

While a template is required for this project, all sides of the pattern piece are straight, which allows you to use your rotary cutter. The Cutting Chart lists the number of strips and their width to cut from the dark and light fabrics, followed by the number of A pieces to cut from those strips. After cutting strips with your rotary-cutting equipment, tape the A template to the underside of a see-through rotary ruler. Align the longest side of the template with the 45 degree line on your ruler, and position the diagonal edge of the template flush with the edge of the ruler, as shown in **Diagram 1.** Then place the template over your fabric strip, as shown, and simply make the final diagonal cut for each A piece. This rotary shortcut will save you from tracing hundreds of A pieces on the black and gray fabrics.

All measurements include ¼-inch seam allowances. Refer to the Cutting Chart for the number of pieces to cut from each fabric.

Note: Cut and piece one sample block before cutting all the fabric for the quilt.

— Sew Easy

The rotary ruler/template method described in "Cutting" can speed up cutting all of the bright print A pieces, too. If you use scraps, you won't have long strips of fabric, but you can still stack a few scraps, cut the layers into 3½-inch-wide strips (even if they are short), and then tape your A template to the ruler as described. You may not be able to cut a dozen A pieces from one set of strips, but even if you cut one or two, you'll save time because your scrap fabrics are layered and you are able to use your rotary cutter.

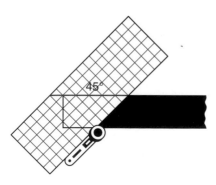

45°

Diagram 1

PIECING THE BLOCKS

Two block variations are used in this quilt to give the light and dark diamond effect in the quilt setting. One block has light gray print pinwheels in the center, and the other has black print pinwheel centers. The placement of the medium prints is the same in both block variations, as shown in the **Block Diagram.**

Gray
Pinwheel

Black
Pinwheel

Block Diagram

Gray Pinwheel Blocks

Step 1. For one gray pinwheel block, you'll need six light gray A pieces, two black A pieces, and eight medium print A pieces. Lay out the fabric into four groups, each containing four pieces, as shown in **Diagram 2A.**

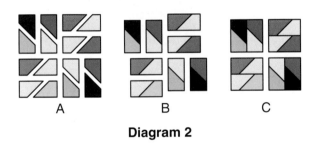

A   B   C

Diagram 2

Step 2. Sew each pair of A pieces together along the diagonal edges, as shown in **2B.** Press the seam allowances toward the darker fabric in each pair.

········ Sew Quick ········

Assembly line piecing can be used to make piecing this quilt top quick and easy. Instead of laying out all your pieces individually, start by sewing each light gray piece to a print piece along the diagonal edge. Keep feeding pairs of light gray and print A pieces through your machine. Then sew each black piece to a print piece along the diagonal edge in the same assembly line manner. When you lay out your pieces, you'll already have Step 2 (above) completed!

Step 3. Sew the two pairs in each quadrant together, as shown in **2C.** Press the seam allowances to one side.

Step 4. Sew the four units together to complete the block. Don't press the seam allowances yet. Repeat until you've assembled the total number of gray Pinwheel blocks required for your quilt size.

Black Pinwheel Blocks

For one black pinwheel block, you'll need six black A pieces, two light gray A pieces, and eight medium print A pieces. In this block, the gray and black pieces are in opposite positions from the light Pinwheel blocks, as shown in **Diagram 3.** Sew these blocks together in the same manner as the gray blocks. Make the total number of black Pinwheel blocks required for your quilt size. Do not press the seams yet.

Diagram 3

ASSEMBLING THE QUILT TOP

Step 1. Following the assembly diagrams on pages 48–49, use a design wall or other flat surface to arrange the quilt blocks for your size quilt into horizontal rows. Press the center seams of adjacent blocks in opposite directions so you can more easily align them for sewing.

Step 2. Sew the blocks in each row together. Press all seams in adjoining rows in opposite directions, then sew the rows together, matching seams carefully. Press the quilt top.

ATTACHING THE MITERED BORDERS

All the action in this quilt is contained within a mitered double border. You will need to sew the

Double-Size Assembly Diagram

inch-wide black border strips. Keep the side border strips separate from those for the top and bottom of the quilt.

Step 3. Working with the side borders first, pin and sew a dark blue border strip and a black border strip together, as shown in **Diagram 4.** Press the seams toward the black border. Repeat with the remaining side border strips. In the same manner, pin and sew the top and bottom border strips together into two units. Press the seams toward the blue border.

Diagram 4

Step 4. Pin and sew the four border units to the quilt top, making sure the narrow blue border is flush with the quilt's edges. Refer to page 119 for instructions on adding borders with mitered corners. When preparing the miters, be sure to match the seams of the strips in adjacent borders, as shown in the **Quilt Diagram** on page 50.

QUILTING AND FINISHING

Step 1. Mark the quilt top for quilting, if desired. The quilt shown was machine quilted in the ditch around each piece. A simple scallop design was used in the outer border as a nice relief from all of the jagged edges in the patchwork.

Step 2. Regardless of which quilt size you've chosen to make, the backing will have to be pieced. For either quilt, cut the backing fabric crosswise into three equal pieces, and trim the selvages. Cut a 35-inch-wide segment from the entire length of two pieces. Sew a narrow segment to each side of the wide piece, as shown in **Diagram 5.**

Step 3. Layer the quilt top, batting, and backing; baste the layers together. Quilt as desired.

dark blue strips to the black strips for each edge of the quilt first, then add them to the quilt top as a single unit, mitering the corners.

Step 1. To determine the length for the side borders, measure the quilt top vertically, taking the measurement through the center of the quilt. To this measurement, add two times the finished width of the border (4 inches × 2 = 8 inches), plus 5 inches. This is the length you will need to make the two side borders. In the same manner, measure the quilt top horizontally through the center and calculate the length of the top and bottom borders.

Step 2. Sew the 1½-inch-wide dark blue border strips together end to end to make strips of the lengths calculated in Step 1. Repeat with the 3½-

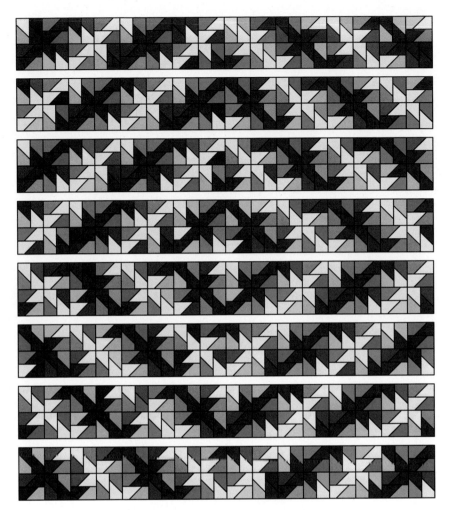

King-Size Assembly Diagram

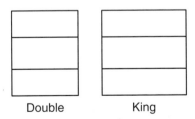

Double   King

Diagram 5

Step 4. Referring to the directions on page 121, make and attach double-fold binding. In the quilt shown, the binding is the same fabric as the outer border. To calculate the amount of binding needed for your quilt size, add the length of the four sides of the quilt plus 9 inches. The total is the approximate number of inches of binding you will need.

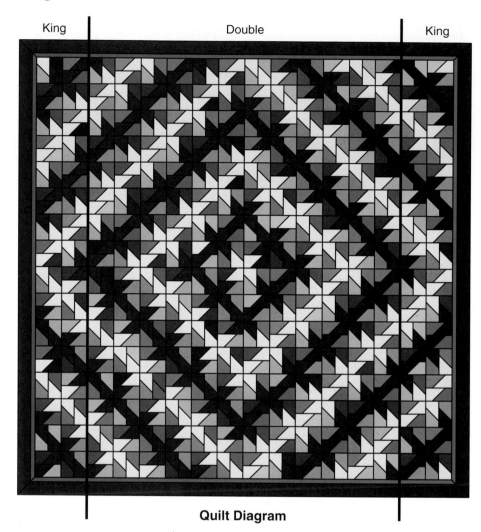

King   Double   King

Quilt Diagram

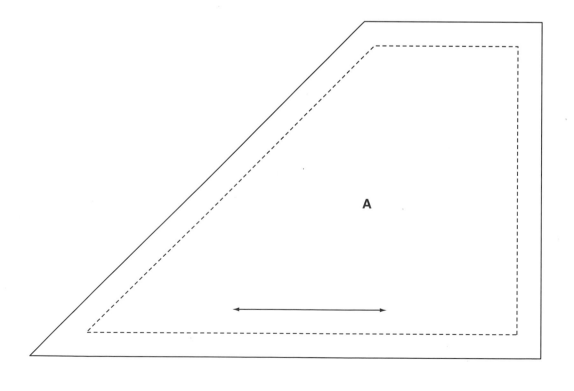

A

BARN RAISING PINWHEELS
Color Plan

Photocopy this page and use it to experiment with color schemes for your quilt.

CHARMING SPOOLS

Skill Level: *Intermediate*

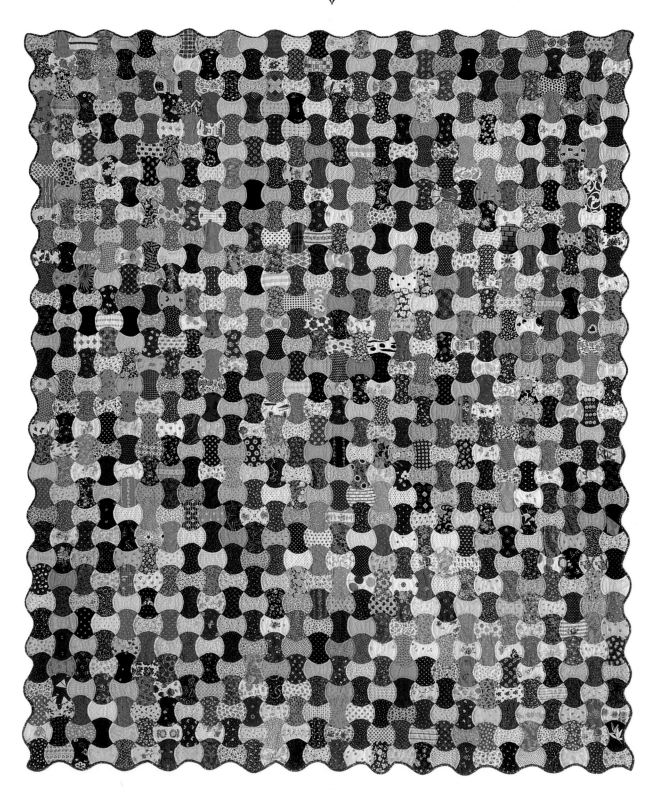

*A*lso known as Double Hammerhead, Double Ax, and Apple Core, this One Patch shape is curved on all four sides. Typically, this shape is hand pieced, as was done by quiltmaker Phyllis Klein, yet it is possible to machine piece the curves with excellent results. This twin-size quilt is arranged in a pattern of alternating light and dark fabrics, and since it's a charm quilt, no fabric is repeated.

BEFORE YOU BEGIN

Although the quiltmaker chose to piece this quilt by hand, you may decide to machine piece your quilt. For either method, see page 108 for more information about sewing curved seams.

CHOOSING FABRICS

The charm quilt shown in the photograph contains 952 different print fabrics—a different one for each spool. All dark spools are positioned vertically in the quilt, and all light spools are placed horizontally. Placement is staggered from row to row, so that each spool is sewn to another of contrasting value. For more information about color value, be sure to read "What Is Color Value" on page 106.

Choose as many fabrics as possible to construct a quilt similar to the one shown. You can make a successful scrap quilt, even if every patch is not unique, by scattering identical fabric pieces across the quilt top. The dark and light yardage requirements given are an estimate based on the total amount of fabric used. For this quilt, however, it is probably

Quilt Sizes		
	Twin (shown)	King
Finished Quilt Size	77½" × 94"	99½" × 99½"
Number of Spools	952	1,296

Materials		
	Twin	King
Assorted dark prints	6 yards	8 yards
Assorted light prints	6 yards	8 yards
Backing	7¼ yards	9⅛ yards
Batting	86" × 102"	108" × 108"
Binding	1 yard	1 yard

NOTE: Yardages are estimates, based on using scraps that measure at least 3½ × 5 inches.

more useful to think of yardage in terms of the number of spools used. For each spool, you need an approximately 3½ × 5-inch scrap of fabric (about the size of a small index card). The Cutting Chart on page 54 lists the number of dark and light spools required for each quilt size.

Just because many One Patch quilts are charm quilts doesn't mean that this quilt pattern only works when each piece is cut from a different fabric. Imagine spools in many shades of blue and white

or perhaps in country reds and greens. Or, instead of alternating dark and light values, try dark and light shading in diagonal rows or creating a rectangle within a rectangle. To create your own color scheme, photocopy the **Color Plan** on page 57, and use crayons or colored pencils to experiment with color choices.

CUTTING

Construct a durable template from the Spool pattern piece on

Cutting Chart

Fabric	Used For	Number to Cut	
		Twin	King
Dark prints	Spools	476	648
Light prints	Spools	476	648

page 56. For hand piecing, mark the seam line and the cutting line. For machine piecing, you only need to mark the outer cutting line. For more information about constructing templates, see page 116. Refer to the Cutting Chart for the number of pieces needed for your size quilt.

Note: Cut and piece a few sample spools before cutting all the fabric for the quilt.

Sew Easy

It's important that your spool template be accurate, yet it can be difficult to trace curved lines by hand. Instead of tracing the entire line, try using a fine-point, permanent, felt-tip pen to make a series of dots on your template plastic, following the line of the pattern underneath. Make your dots about ⅛ inch apart. After dotting your way around the entire pattern, simply cut out following the dots. You'll be surprised at how smooth and accurate your template is.

ASSEMBLING THE SPOOLS

A design wall is a great help for laying out this type of quilt. To construct a simple design area, tack pieces of flannel to a wall. The fabric pieces will stick to the flannel without being pinned and can be repositioned quickly and easily until you are pleased with the layout. Then pieces can be pinned so they remain in place until you're ready to sew them together.

Working with the entire quilt layout is best, but if space prohibits this, lay out the quilt in sections, then sew the completed sections together.

Step 1. Referring to the photograph on page 52 or the **Quilt Diagram** on page 56, lay out as many rows as possible for your quilt size, alternating light and dark pieces, as shown. The twin-size quilt has 34 rows of 28 spools each, and the king-size quilt has 36 rows of 36 spools each. Notice that adjoining rows begin and end with spools of contrasting value.

Step 2. When you are satisfied with the color and value placement of your quilt layout, begin sewing pieces together, as shown in **Diagram 1**. With right sides facing, pin two spools together, matching centers and outside edges. Hand or machine stitch the pieces together. If you are machine stitching, sew with the concave curve on top, as shown. Having this piece on top makes it easier to stretch it as needed to fit the convex curve of the other spool. Press the seam to one side, as shown in **Diagram 2**. For more information about hand piecing curved seams, see Charmed Ogee on page 76.

Match centers   Pin curves to fit

Diagram 1

Diagram 2

Step 3. Add the required number of spools to complete one row, referring to the **Partial Assembly Diagram,** and continue until all rows have been completed.

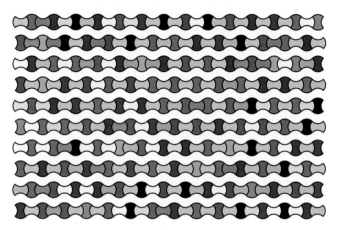

Partial Assembly Diagram

Step 4. Sew the rows together, matching seams and easing curves to fit. Press all seams between rows in the same direction.

Sew Easy

If you find it awkward to work with such long rows of spools, you may want to try piecing spools together in a four patch arrangement, as shown. Join pieces 1 and 2, then pieces 3 and 4. Then join the pairs using one long, gently curving seam line. After the four-spool units are assembled, simply stitch them together into rows.

Seam line to join
pairs of spools

QUILTING AND FINISHING

Step 1. Mark the quilt top for quilting, if desired. All of the light spools in the quilt shown were outline quilted ¼ inch from their seams, making the dark spools stand out. Or try an allover quilting motif such as Baptist fans or single, double, or triple cross-hatching for a completely different look.

Step 2. Regardless of which quilt size you've chosen to make, the backing will have to be pieced. For the twin-size quilt, cut the backing fabric crosswise into three equal pieces, and trim the selvages. Cut a 31-inch-wide panel from two of the pieces, then sew one of these panels to each side of the full-width piece, as shown in **Diagram 3.** Press the seams open.

Twin   King

Diagram 3

Step 3. For the king-size quilt, cut the backing fabric crosswise into three equal pieces, and trim the selvages. Cut a 34-inch-wide panel from two of the pieces. Sew one of these panels to each side of the full-width piece, as shown. Press the seams open.

Step 4. Layer the quilt top, batting, and backing, and baste the layers together. Quilt as desired.

Step 5. Because of all of the curves along the outer edges of this quilt, bias binding will work best. See page 110 for information about applying binding around curves. You'll need approximately 460 inches of bias binding for the twin-size quilt and approximately 535 inches for the king-size quilt. Or, if you prefer, hand finish your quilt without binding, as described in "Finishing without Binding" on page 111.

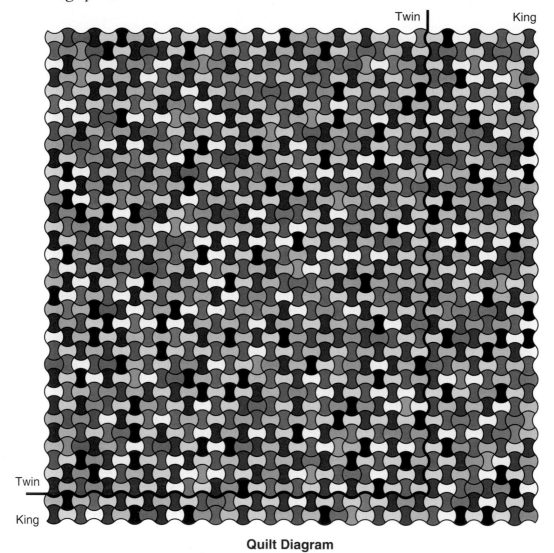

Quilt Diagram

Spool

CHARMING SPOOLS
Color Plan

Photocopy this page and use it to experiment with color schemes for your quilt.

THOUSAND PYRAMIDS

Skill Level: *Easy*

*L*egend has it that charm quilts have 999 different pieces, which may be where the name Thousand Pyramids came from. Yet in reality, neither the quilt shown here nor most other charm quilts have 999 pieces. Thousand Pyramids is a classic One Patch design and is suited to just about all skill levels and either hand or machine piecing. Missouri quiltmaker Bettina Havig, who made this double-size charm quilt, effectively limited her palette to teal, peach, and black prints and still managed to have no two pieces the same!

BEFORE YOU BEGIN

The quiltmaker pieced this quilt by hand. You may decide that you would prefer to machine piece. In addition to the directions provided here for piecing, see page 116 for more information on both machine and hand piecing techniques.

Whether you choose to hand or machine piece, you will need to make templates for pieces A and B from the patterns on page 64, as described in "Cutting" on page 60.

CHOOSING FABRICS

The interior of this quilt is actually a charm quilt, with each pyramid cut from a different fabric. The colors of these pieces are closely related and selected from a limited number of color families. Teal, black, peach, rust, and off-white prints are predominant. To create a similar visual effect in your quilt, start by selecting the basic color families you want to feature. Within those families, you will need to choose as many fabrics as possible from

at least four different color values (light, medium light, medium, and dark). This quilt will work equally well as a scrap quilt of many diverse colors or as one with a planned color scheme, as long as you can separate your fabrics into these four color

values. For more information about color value, see page 106.

To help develop your own color scheme, photocopy the **Color Plan** on page 65, and use colored pencils or crayons to experiment with different color combinations.

Quilt Sizes

	Double (shown)	Queen
Finished Quilt Size	79" × 88"	92" × 101½"

Materials

	Double	Queen
Assorted light prints	1¾ yards	2½ yards
Assorted medium light prints	1¼ yards	1⅞ yards
Assorted medium prints	1¼ yards	1⅞ yards
Assorted dark prints	4 yards	6 yards
Dark teal print	1⅝ yards	1¾ yards
Medium green print	1 yard	1⅛ yards
Navy print	⅝ yard	¾ yard
Backing	7⅜ yards	8½ yards
Batting	87" × 96"	100" × 110"
Binding	¾ yard	⅞ yard

NOTE: Yardages are based on 44/45-inch-wide fabrics that are at least 42 inches wide after preshrinking.

Cutting Chart

Fabric	Used For	Piece	Number to Cut	
			Double	Queen
Light prints	Pyramids	A	140	206
	Half-pyramids	B	4	4
	Half-pyramids	B reverse	4	4
Medium light prints	Pyramids	A	105	155
	Half-pyramids	B	3	4
	Half-pyramids	B reverse	3	4
Medium prints	Pyramids	A	105	155
	Half-pyramids	B	3	4
	Half-pyramids	B reverse	3	4
Dark prints	Pyramids	A	350	516
	Half-pyramids	B	10	12
	Half-pyramids	B reverse	10	12

Fabric	Used For	Strip Width	Number to Cut	
			Double	Queen
Navy print	Inner border	2"	9	10
Medium green print	Middle border	3½"	9	10
Dark teal print	Outer border	6"	9	10

CUTTING

All measurements include ¼-inch seam allowances. Refer to the Cutting Chart for the types and number of pieces you must cut from templates A, B, and B reverse.

Construct durable templates of pattern pieces A and B, as they will be used to cut many pieces. Use the B template to cut the B reverse pieces by turning it over. For hand piecing, mark the seam line and the cutting line. For machine piecing, only the cutting line is necessary. To make alignment easier, the tips of the pyramid ends have been trimmed from the patterns, removing the excess seam allowance. For more information about constructing templates, see page 116.

Note: Cut and piece a few sample pyramids before cutting all the fabric for the quilt.

LAYING OUT THE PYRAMIDS

As with the construction of most other One Patch quilts, a design wall is beneficial, since it allows you an overall view of the work in progress. To construct a simple design area, tack pieces of flannel to a wall. Pieces will stick to the flannel readily, and they can be repositioned quickly and easily or pinned in place when you are happy with the arrangement.

The design process for this quilt will likely be one of trial and error, where pyramids are moved about until the layout suits you. Don't let this task overwhelm you. Take your time and enjoy how fun and freeing this can be when you don't worry about matching fabrics of the pyramids that touch each other. It's the overall effect of the quilt top that's important.

— Sew Easy —

While the grain line is marked on the A and B pattern pieces, you don't need to worry too much about the fabric grain. If you have small scraps that will only accommodate the shape of the pyramid when the template isn't laid on the straight of grain, you can still use them. Since the angle of the pyramid is not on a true bias (45 degree angle), you won't experience a great deal of stretch in your pieces. So go ahead and use all of your scraps, even if they can't be cut on the straight of grain. If possible, however, cut the B pieces with the right-angled edges along the grain, since these will be the outside edges of the quilt top, and you'll want them to be more stable.

alternate rows. Position the B and B reverse half-pyramids now to complete each dark row.

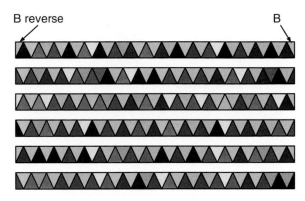

Partial Assembly Diagram

Step 1. When you look at the photograph on page 58, you'll notice that all of the dark pyramids point upward. To construct a quilt similar to the one shown, begin your layout by placing a dark pyramid in all of those positions, lining them up one after another in rows, as shown in **Diagram 1**, with the bases of the pyramids in each row parallel and touching. Notice that pyramids in one row are staggered halfway between those in adjoining rows. For the double-size quilt, you will have 18 dark A pyramids in the first row, and in the queen-size quilt, you will have 22.

Diagram 1

Step 2. Continue building your quilt rows, laying out the number of dark pyramids required in each row, as shown in the **Partial Assembly Diagram.** A dark half-pyramid, cut from B or B reverse, appears at the beginning and end of

Step 3. Referring again to the photograph, notice that the pyramids that point downward are a mixture of the light and medium value fabrics. Begin placing fabric pyramids in the downward position, as shown in **Diagram 2.** For a quilt similar to the one in the photograph, refer to the values shown in the **Quilt Diagram** on page 63 as a guide. After placing the lighter A pyramids, position the light and medium B and B reverse half-pyramids to finish laying out all of the rows.

Diagram 2

Step 4. When the initial layout on your design wall is complete, step back and take a look at your quilt. Reposition pyramids until you have a design that you are satisfied with. You will likely find that a few of the dark and light pyramids need to be repositioned, but don't be concerned about carefully matching all of the fabrics.

Step 5. To begin assembling the rows, align two neighboring A pyramids, as shown in **Diagram 3** on page 61, and sew them together. Press the seam toward the darker pyramid. Continue adding pyramids until an entire horizontal row has been completed. Sew the B and B reverse half-pyramids to the row ends in the same manner.

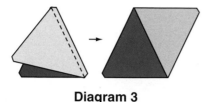

Diagram 3

Step 6. When all rows are completed, sew them together, matching seams carefully where pyramids meet. Press all seams in the same direction.

ADDING THE MITERED BORDERS

This quilt has a 1½-inch navy print inner border, a 3-inch medium green middle border, and a 5½-inch dark teal outer border. The three strips for each quilt edge are sewn together first, then added to the quilt top as a single unit with mitered corners.

Step 1. To determine the correct length for the side borders, measure the quilt top vertically through the center. To this measurement, add two times the finished width of the border (10 inches × 2 = 20 inches), plus 5 inches. This is the length you will need to make the two side borders. In the same manner, measure the quilt top horizontally through the center, and add twice the width of the borders to calculate the length of the top and bottom borders.

Step 2. Sew the navy border strips together end to end until you've achieved the required lengths for each border. Keep the side border strips separate from those for the top and bottom of the quilt. Repeat, sewing together the green border strips and the teal border strips to achieve the lengths needed for your quilt.

Step 3. To make the side borders, pin and sew the navy, green, and teal strips together lengthwise, with the green strips in the center, as shown in **Diagram 4**. Press the seams toward the outer border. In the same manner, pin and sew the top

and bottom border strips together. Press the seams toward the inner border.

Diagram 4

Step 4. Pin and sew the navy edges of the border units to the quilt top, referring to page 119 for complete instructions on adding borders with mitered corners. When preparing the miters, be sure to match like strips in adjacent borders, as shown in the **Quilt Diagram.**

QUILTING AND FINISHING

Step 1. Mark the quilt top for quilting, if desired. In the quilt shown, all pyramids were outline quilted ¼ inch from the seams. The borders were quilted with a series of diagonal lines to repeat the pyramid theme.

Step 2. Regardless of which quilt size you've chosen to make, the backing will have to be pieced. For the double-size quilt, cut the backing fabric crosswise into three equal lengths, and trim the selvages. Cut a 28-inch-wide panel from two of the pieces, then sew one of these narrow panels to each side of the full-width panel, as shown in **Diagram 5.** Press the seams open.

Diagram 5

Step 3. For the queen-size quilt, cut the backing fabric crosswise into three equal lengths, and trim the selvages. Cut a 35-inch-wide panel

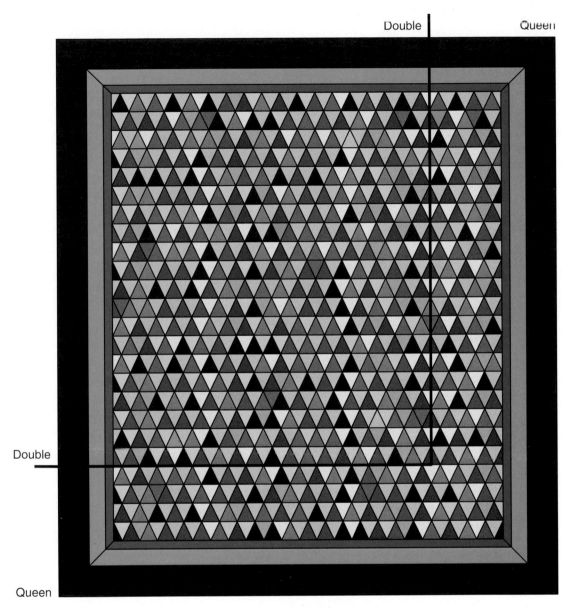

Double | Queen

Double

Queen

Quilt Diagram

from two of the pieces, then sew one of the narrower panels to each side of the full-width panel, as shown. Press the seams open.

Step 4. Layer the quilt top, batting, and backing, and baste the layers together. Quilt as desired.

Step 5. Referring to the directions on page 121, make and attach double-fold binding. To calculate the amount of binding needed for your quilt size, add the length of the four sides of the quilt plus 9 inches. The total is the approximate number of inches of binding you will need.

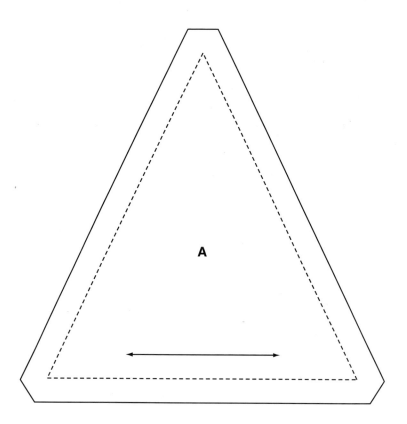

A

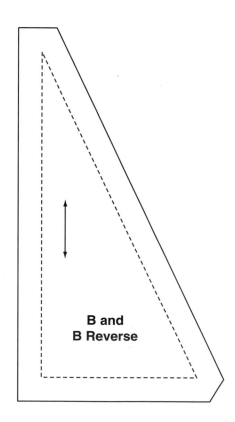

**B and
B Reverse**

Thousand Pyramids
Color Plan

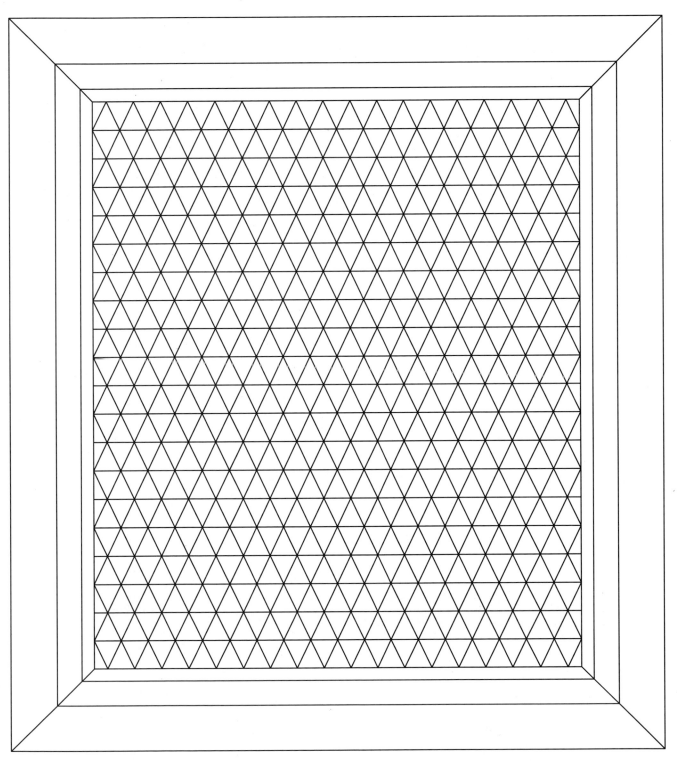

Photocopy this page and use it to experiment with color schemes for your quilt.

SIMPLY CHARMING

Skill Level: *Advanced*

A divided 60 degree diamond and careful placement of color value allows an occasional six-pointed star to peek out from among the more traditional tumbling blocks in this quilt. And that's just the effect quiltmaker Edith Zimmer had in mind when she made some split diamonds of contrasting values and others of the same color value. Whether you see stars or tumbling blocks, Edith guarantees you won't see two of the same fabric in this twin-size charm quilt.

BEFORE YOU BEGIN

To eliminate the distortion that can take place when handling and sewing together long, thin triangles with bias edges, the pieced diamonds are made by stitching two rectangles together first. Then a template is used to cut the diamond shape from the already-pieced fabric. This technique will save lots of time in cutting and tracing and allow for greater accuracy in piecing. While making the diamonds is easy, the quilt has many set-in seams, which make it a more challenging project to complete. The real challenge, however, is in placing the colors and fabrics to achieve the effect of stars and tumbling blocks. So, if you are comfortable with sewing set-in seams and are looking for a fun project to stimulate your sense of color, this is the perfect one.

CHOOSING FABRICS

The quilt shown is a charm quilt, so no two pieces are cut from the same fabric. While this pattern does not have to be a charm quilt to be effective, choosing as many fabrics as possible from at least three different color values—light, medium, and dark—will make your quilt design more effective. For more information about color value, see "What Is Color Value?" on page 106.

This quilt is a great project for using the scraps you've been collecting, since each rectangle used to assemble the diamonds measures only 3 × 9 inches. Smaller scrap pieces can be used for the half-diamond shapes and the filler triangles surrounding the outer edges of the quilt.

Quilt Size	
Finished Quilt Size	74¾" × 97¼"
Finished Diamond Size	5" × 8¾"

NOTE: *Due to the complexity of the design, no size variations are provided.*

Materials	
	Amount
Assorted light prints	4⅞ yards
Assorted medium prints	4⅛ yards
Assorted dark prints	4⅛ yards
Border fabric	1 yard
Backing	5⅞ yards
Batting	83" × 106"
Binding	¾ yard

NOTE: *Yardages are based on 44/45-inch-wide fabrics that are at least 42 inches wide after preshrinking.*

Cutting Chart			
Fabric	**Used For**	**Size or Piece**	**Number to Cut**
Light prints	A diamonds	3" × 9"	262
	B triangles	3" × 5"	14
	C triangles	C	8
	D triangle	D	1
	D reverse triangle	D	1
Medium prints	A diamonds	3" × 9"	222
	B triangles	3" × 5"	14
	C triangles	C	8
Dark prints	A diamonds	3" × 9"	222
	B triangles	3" × 5"	14
	C triangles	C	8
Border fabric	Border	3" strips	10

The quiltmaker made approximately one-quarter of her diamonds with two contrasting fabrics. The remaining diamonds were sewn with two different fabrics of the same basic color value (two lights, two mediums, or two darks, for example). The different combinations gave her the opportunity to experiment with color and value as she designed the quilt top.

The Cutting Chart lists suggested numbers of 3 × 9-inch rectangles to cut from three color values to make a quilt similar to the one shown. If you would like to change the layout, use the **Color Plan** on page 73 to devise your own design, then count the number of rectangles you'll need from each value combination used. To give you more design options when laying out the quilt, make a few extra diamonds in all value combinations.

CUTTING

All measurements include ¼-inch seam allowances. Refer to the Cutting Chart for the types and number of pieces you need to cut. Construct transparent plastic templates of pattern pieces A, B, C, and D on pages 74–75. Be sure to mark the center seam lines on your A and B templates so you can easily align them with the seams in your fabric.

Half-diamonds, cut from template B, are used as fillers around the side edges of the quilt. Template C is the same triangle found in the pieced diamonds, but it is used to cut the single triangles that fill spaces around the top and bottom edges of the quilt. Template D triangles are used in the bottom corners of the quilt. You will need a total of 14 B triangles, 17 C triangles, and 2 D triangles. Note that the Cutting Chart instructs you to cut extras of these pieces. This way, when you're laying out your quilt, you can decide if you need a light, medium, or dark triangle to suit your quilt top. For more information about making and using templates, see page 116.

Note: Cut and assemble a few pieced diamonds to test your templates before cutting all the fabric for the quilt.

MAKING SPLIT DIAMONDS

Step 1. Sew two 3 × 9-inch rectangles together lengthwise. Press the seam to one side. Align the seam line on template A along the seam line of your pieced rectangles, as shown in **Diagram 1.** Mark around the template, then use scissors or rotary-cutting equipment to cut out the diamond shape on the lines, as shown.

Sew rectangles together

Trace around diamond template

Cut out diamond

Diagram 1

Assembly Diagram. You may also want to refer to the **Quilt Diagram** on page 72 or the photograph on page 66 for ideas on color placement, or feel free to experiment with your own ideas.

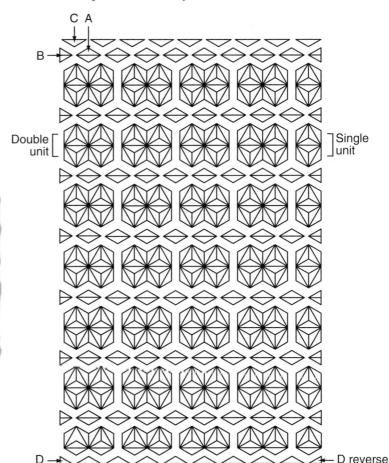

Assembly Diagram

Sew Quick

For quick and accurate cutting, use your rotary cutter and ruler to cut out the diamonds after they have been marked on your fabric. Simply align your ruler with the drawn line and slice away the corner.

Step 2. Repeat with all remaining rectangles to make the number of each split diamond combination listed in **Diagram 2**.

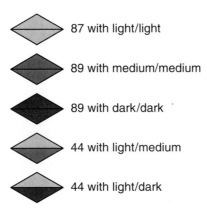

87 with light/light

89 with medium/medium

89 with dark/dark

44 with light/medium

44 with light/dark

Diagram 2

LAYING OUT THE QUILT TOP

Step 1. Use a design wall or other flat surface to lay out the diamonds into rows, as shown in the

Sew Easy

Save the four corner triangles that you trim from each rectangle, and you'll have a head start on your next scrap quilt!

Step 2. When you are satisfied with the layout, begin sewing the A diamonds together, as shown in **Diagram 3** on page 70. First sew together two pairs of diamonds, as shown in **3A**, starting and stopping your seams 1/4 inch from each end of the diamonds. This will enable you to set in connecting diamonds. Next, sew the horizontal diamond that separates the two pairs to one of the pairs, as shown in **3B**, pivoting at the corner and starting and stopping ¼ inch from each end of the seam. Attach the other pair of diamonds to the bottom of the horizontal diamond in the same manner, so your unit looks like **3C**.

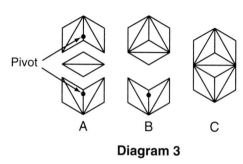

Pivot

A   B   C

Diagram 3

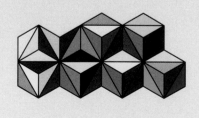

·········Sew Quick·········

The layout of your quilt is entirely up to you. If you want more stars to appear, arrange diamonds with high contrast in color value in a clockwise fashion so that the dark half of one diamond touches the light half of the diamond next to it. Continue laying out dark/light diamonds in a clockwise fashion, as in the left side of the diagram.

If you want to build more tumbling blocks, simply make more diamonds with similar values, then arrange them with light diamonds on top, dark diamonds on the bottom right, and medium diamonds on the bottom left, as shown in the right side of the diagram.

Step 3. Make another unit like the one shown in **3C**. Sew the two units together, as shown in **Diagram 4**. Repeat to make 24 such units, referring to the **Assembly Diagram** on page 69. The right end of each horizontal row has the single unit made in **3C**. You will need six of these units.

Diagram 4

Step 4. To complete the sides of the quilt, make 14 B half-diamonds. Referring to your layout, determine the color value for each side of each half-diamond. Then sew pairs of the 3 × 5-inch rectangles together lengthwise. Align your B template with the seam on each rectangle, as shown in **Diagram 5**. Mark around the template and cut out the triangle on the line. Place the B triangles in your quilt layout along the side edges. See the **Assembly Diagram**.

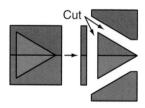

Cut

Diagram 5

Step 5. Referring again to the **Assembly Diagram**, lay out 17 of the C triangles around the top and bottom edges of your quilt. You will have leftover C pieces. D and D reverse pieces will be used to complete the bottom corners of the quilt top.

Step 6. Referring to the **Row Assembly Diagram**, sew the units into rows, leaving ¼ inch open at each end of the seams. The rows will have a zigzag formation, so that fewer set-in seams will need to be sewn.

Row Assembly Diagram

Step 2. In the same manner, measure the quilt top horizontally through the center, then calculate the length of the top and bottom borders. Piece together the remaining border strips to achieve two borders this length.

Step 3. The borders on this quilt are mitered, as shown in the **Quilt Diagram** on page 72. Center, pin, and sew the borders to the quilt edges, referring to page 119 for instructions on adding borders with mitered corners.

QUILTING AND FINISHING

Step 1. Mark the quilt top for quilting, if desired. The quilt shown has an X quilted in each pieced diamond. The diamonds were also quilted in the ditch.

Step 2. The quilt backing must be pieced, as shown in **Diagram 6.** Cut the backing fabric crosswise into two equal pieces, and trim the selvages. Cut one piece in half lengthwise, and sew a narrow panel to each side of the full-width piece, as shown. Press the seams open.

Diagram 6

Step 7. Sew the rows together, pivoting and setting in seams where the horizontal diamonds link units in adjoining rows. For more information about set-in seams, see page 108. Press the quilt top.

ADDING THE MITERED BORDERS

Step 1. To determine the length of the side borders, measure the quilt top vertically through the center and add two times the finished width of the border ($2\frac{1}{2}$ inches $\times$ 2 = 5 inches), plus 5 inches, to this measurement. Piece together the border strips to achieve two borders this length.

Step 3. Layer the quilt top, batting, and backing, and baste the layers together. Quilt all marked designs and add any additional quilting as desired.

Step 4. Referring to the directions on page 121, make and attach double-fold binding. To calculate the amount of binding needed, add the length of the four sides of the quilt plus 9 inches. The total is the approximate number of inches of binding you will need.

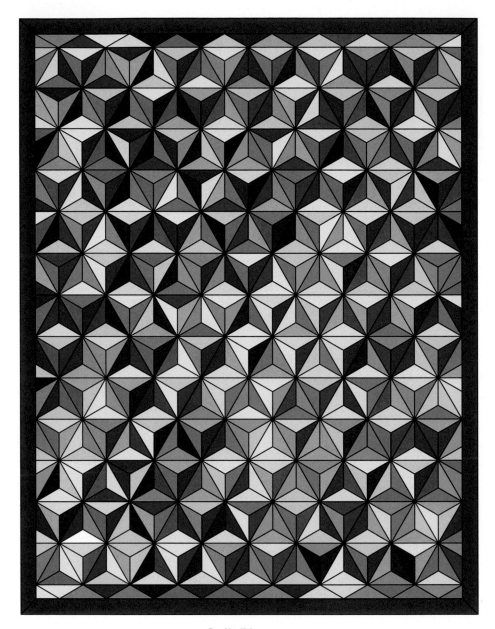

Quilt Diagram

SIMPLY CHARMING
Color Plan

Photocopy this page and use it to experiment with color schemes for your quilt.

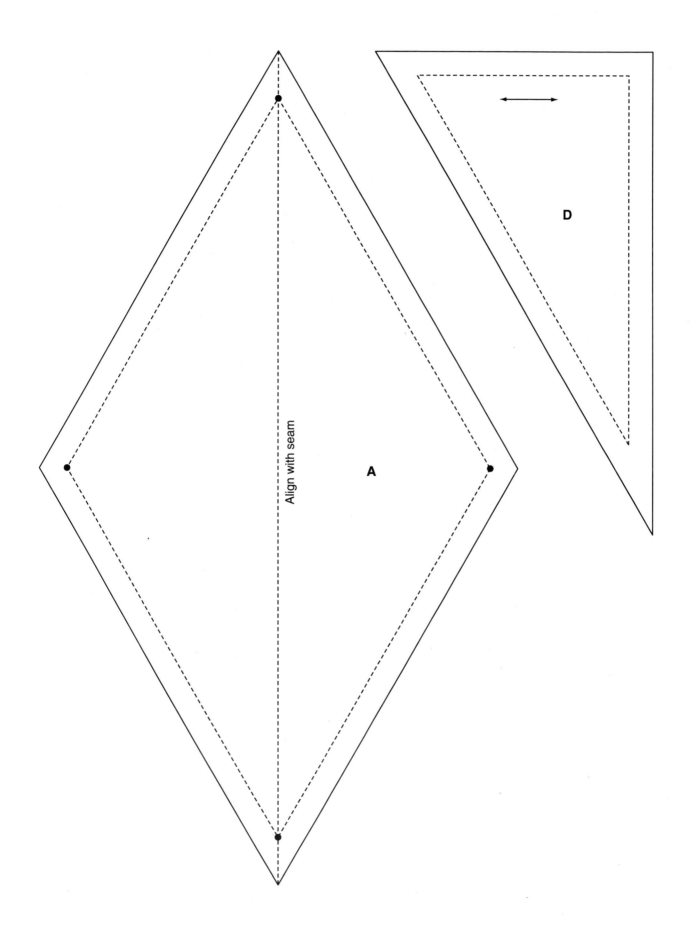

Align with seam

A

D

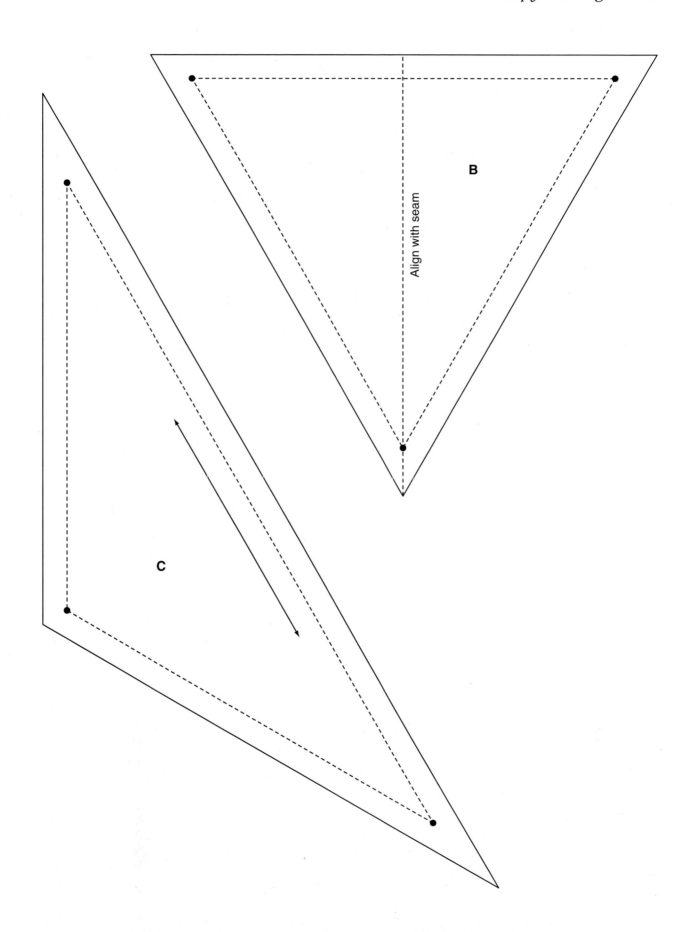

Align with seam

B

C

Charmed Ogee

Skill Level: *Intermediate*

Quiltmaker Julia Zgliniec's unusual wallhanging grew out of her visits to charm square exchange meetings at two different quilt guilds. The ogee (the official name for a curving unit with an S-profile) is made with the basic clamshell shape, which, when pieced into units of four, also happens to look just like an ogee-shape arch.

BEFORE YOU BEGIN

The shells are sewn together in groups of four, which are then sewn into diagonal rows to simplify placing the dark and light fabrics in their proper positions. The navy ogees in the outer ring of the quilt shown are cut from a single, larger template.

The instructions are written for hand piecing, but machine piecing is an option if you feel comfortable machine sewing curves. Centering points are marked on the patterns along cutting and seam lines to help align fabrics for hand or machine piecing.

Make window templates from pattern pieces A, B, C, D, and E on pages 81–82, so that you can mark both seam lines and cutting lines. Be sure to transfer centering marks to your templates. For more information on window templates, see page 110.

Quilt Sizes

	Wallhanging (shown)	Double
Finished Quilt Size	47" × 55"	95" × 119"
Number of Pieced Units		
Dark	12	108
Light	20	130

Materials

	Wallhanging	Double
Dark prints	⅜ yard	3 yards
Medium dark prints	⅜ yard	3 yards
Medium prints	½ yard	3½ yards
Light prints	½ yard	3½ yards
Navy solid	1 yard	2¼ yards
Dark rust print	⅞ yard	1¾ yards
Backing	3⅛ yards	8¾ yards
Batting	55" × 63"	103" × 127"
Binding	⅜ yard	⅞ yard
Freezer paper		

NOTE: Yardages are based on 44/45-inch-wide fabrics that are at least 42 inches wide after preshrinking.

CHOOSING FABRICS

Bring out your scrap basket for this quilt, and sort pieces into piles of differing values. You'll need four color values for the pieced ogees: dark, medium dark, medium, and light. Don't worry about color; just focus on the color value. Since value placement is an important ingredient in this quilt, be sure to read "What Is Color Value" on page 106.

For the A clamshell, you'll need squares that measure at least 4½ inches after prewashing.

CUTTING

All patterns and strip measurements include ¼-inch seam allowances. Refer to the Cutting Chart on page 78 for the number of pieces to cut for the quilt size you are making.

Cutting Chart

Fabric	Used For	Piece	Number to Cut Wallhanging	Double
Dark prints	Clamshells	A	24	216
Medium dark prints	Clamshells	A	24	216
Medium prints	Clamshells	A	40	260
Light prints	Clamshells	A	40	260
Navy solid	Outer ogees	B	18	46
Rust print	Side fillers	C	10	26
	Top and bottom fillers	D	8	20
	Corners	E	2	2
	Corners	E reverse	2	2
	Borders	4" strips	5	10

To cut the fabric shells, trace template A onto the wrong side of each fabric, tracing around both the outer and the inner edges of the window template. Cut out the shells on the outer lines only. You will also need to cut finished-size shells (the inside of the window template) from freezer paper. Since the freezer paper templates can be reused several times, you will not have to cut as many of these.

The outer navy pieces are the same size as a four-shell unit, but they are cut from template B. Mark the seam line and centering points on the right side of each fabric piece. Cut an equal number of freezer paper B pieces using the inside edge of the window template.

The rust side filler pieces are cut from the same fabric as the border with templates C, D, and E. Cut the C and D pieces as you did for A and B. Cut the same number of C and D pieces from freezer paper as you do from fabric, marking around the inside edge of the template.

Trace along the outside edge of the template to make two E corner pieces, then flip the template over and cut two E reverse pieces. Cut two E and two E reverse pieces from freezer paper as well.

Note: Cut and piece a sample four-shell unit before cutting all the fabric for the quilt.

PIECING THE UNITS

Each pieced unit is composed of four A shells. Two color value layouts are needed: a dark unit and a light unit, as shown in **Diagram 1.**

The dark unit is assembled with the convex edge of two dark-fabric shells facing outward. Two medium dark shells are positioned with their convex edges pointed toward the unit's center. In the light unit, the convex edges of the lightest fabric shells face outward, while the convex edges of the medium fabric shells face inward.

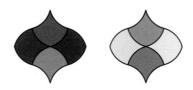

Diagram 1.

Dark Units

Step 1. Center a freezer paper shell, waxy side up, on the wrong side of two dark and two medium dark fabric shells, and pin in place. See **Diagram 2.** Use the tip of a medium hot, dry iron to press the convex edge of the shell onto the freezer paper. Repeat with all shells. See **Diagram 3.**

Diagram 2 **Diagram 3**

Step 2. As shown in **Diagram 4**, position the four shells with right sides up, with the finished edges of the medium dark shells overlapping the concave raw edges of the dark shells. Finished edges should match the seam lines on the concave curves of the dark shells. Use your fingers to feel where each piece of paper ends, then butt the finished curves against the paper pieces. Pin or baste the shells together securely to retain their positions.

Diagram 4

Step 3. Blindstitch the pressed edge of both medium dark shells to the raw edges of the dark shells. Repeat to make all of the dark units for your quilt.

Light Units

The light ogee units are constructed in exactly the same manner as the dark ones. The edges of light fabric shells are left raw, as are the darkest pieces in the dark shells, while the convex edges

of medium-fabric shells are pressed onto freezer paper. Position shells as shown in **Diagram 1**. Make all light ogees required for your quilt size.

ASSEMBLING THE QUILT TOP

The four-shell units, navy B pieces, and rust C and D pieces are positioned into diagonal rows.

Step 1. Center a freezer paper piece, waxy side up, on the wrong side of the B, C, and D pieces; pin.

Step 2. Use a design wall or other flat surface to arrange your quilt into diagonal rows, as shown in the **Wallhanging Assembly Diagram.**

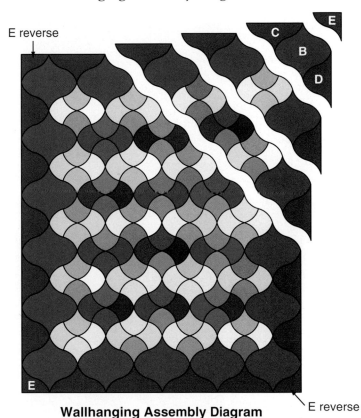

Wallhanging Assembly Diagram

Step 3. Beginning at the top corner of each diagonal row, press the seam allowance on the curved edges of the filler piece under as you did with the shells. Align and blindstitch the pressed edge to the connecting side of a navy B piece. Press under the curved edge of D, and align and stitch it to the opposite side of B. Continue piecing the rows by pressing under the edges and aligning the pieces with the seam line of the connecting pieces or units. Repeat for all rows.

Step 4. Sew the rows together in a similar manner. Press one seam under, then overlap, align, and sew it to the raw edge of the next row.

Step 5. Overlap, align, and stitch an E or E reverse to each corner. Remove all freezer papers.

ADDING THE BORDER

Step 1. Measure the quilt top vertically through the center. Add two times the finished width of the border (3½ inches × 2 = 7 inches), plus 5 inches, to this measurement. Sew rust border strips together end to end to achieve two side borders this length.

Step 2. In the same manner, measure the quilt top horizontally through the center, and calculate the length of the top and bottom borders. Sew the remaining rust border strips together end to end to make two borders this length.

Step 3. Sew the borders to the quilt top, referring to page 119 for instructions on finishing the miters. See the **Double-Size Quilt Diagram.**

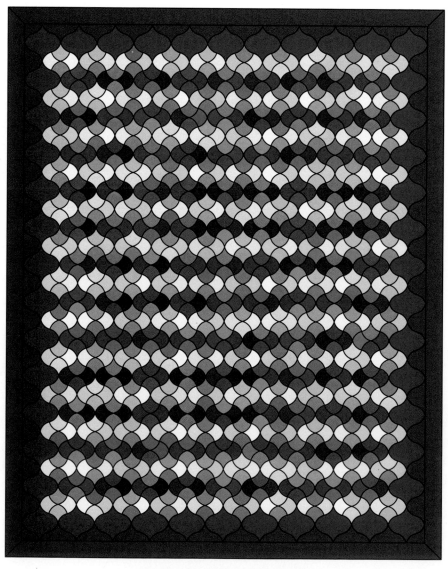

Double-Size Quilt Diagram

QUILTING AND FINISHING

Step 1. Mark the quilt top for quilting. The quilt shown was quilted in the ditch around the shells. Outline quilting was used around each of the navy pieces.

Step 2. For either size quilt, the backing will have to be pieced. For the wallhanging, cut the backing fabric in half crosswise, and trim the selvages. Sew the two pieces together along their long edges, as shown in **Diagram 5.** Press the seams open.

For the double-size quilt, cut the backing fabric in half crosswise, and trim the selvages. Cut one piece in half lengthwise, and sew a narrow panel to each side of the full-width panel, as shown. Press the seams open.

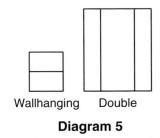

Wallhanging   Double

Diagram 5

Step 3. Layer the quilt top, batting, and backing, and baste. Quilt as desired.

Step 4. Referring to the directions on page 121, make and attach double-fold binding. To calculate the approximate number of inches of binding you will need, add the length of the four sides of the quilt plus 9 inches.

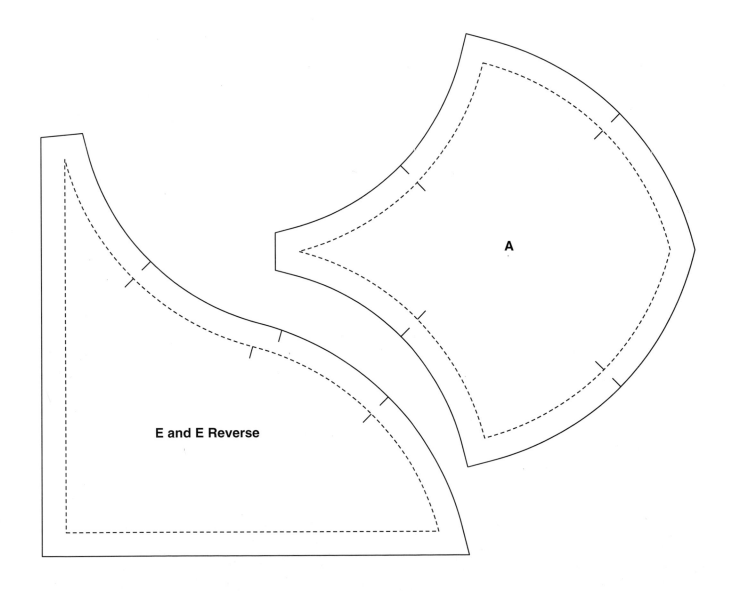

E and E Reverse

A

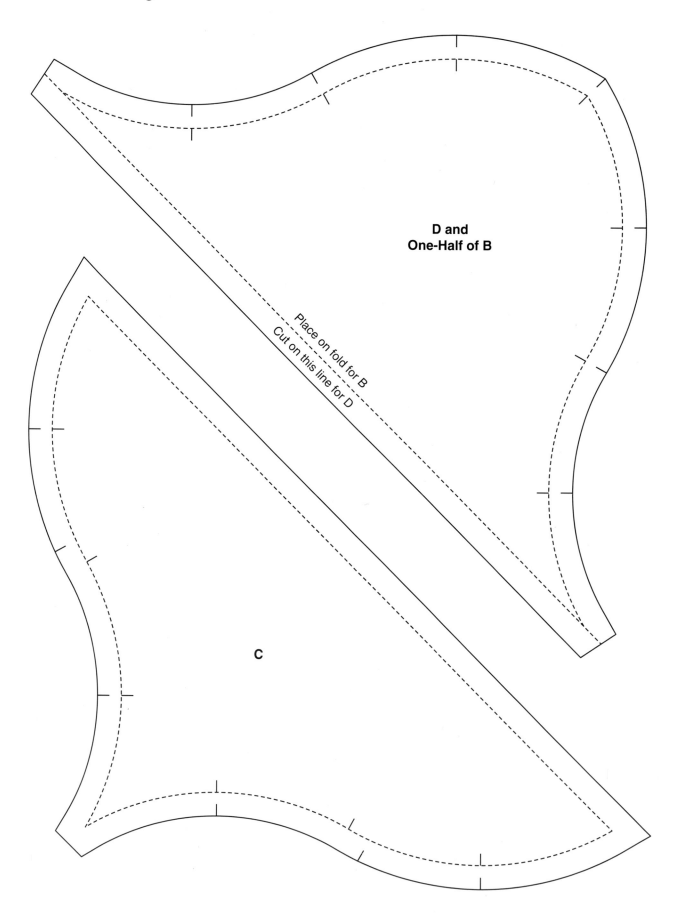

**D and
One-Half of B**

Place on fold for B

Cut on this line for D

C

CHARMED OGEE
Color Plan

Photocopy this page and use it to experiment with color schemes for your quilt.

EVENING AT THE LILY POND

Skill Level: *Challenging*

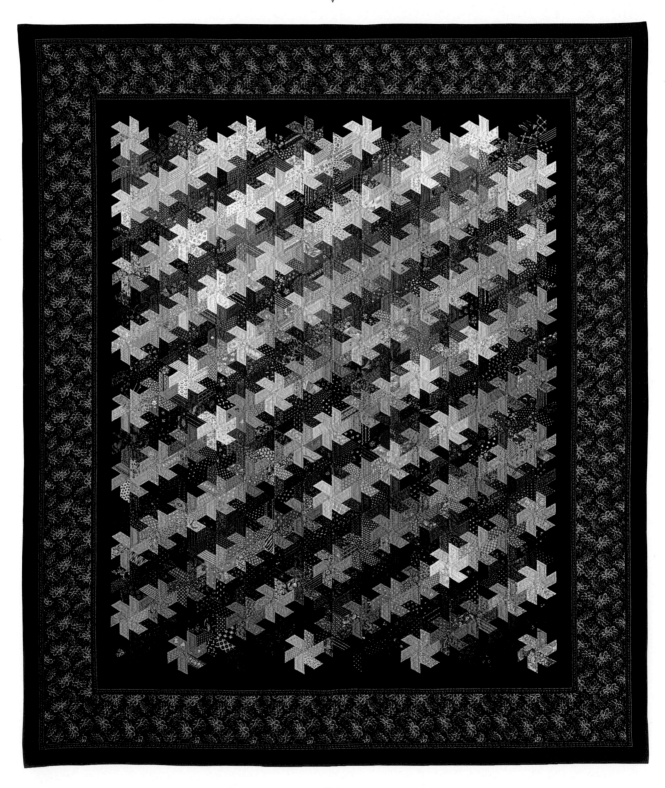

What a wonderful explosion of color! Kathyrn Kuhn artfully arranged hundreds of blue, green, purple, teal, magenta, and black print trapezoids into this gem of a quilt. Reminiscent of the Kansas Twister or Whirligig quilt patterns of the 1930s, her Lily Pond quilt evokes the feel of both water and movement. As for her inspiration, Kathryn admits that an article on tessellations in a math teachers' magazine was what sparked the idea for this double-size quilt.

BEFORE YOU BEGIN

Tessellating half-hexagons form a pinwheel design when stitched together. To achieve this design, it is important to arrange all of the pieces on a design wall or other flat surface before sewing them together. When the layout is complete, the pieces are then sewn together in groups of three to form 60 degree equilateral triangles. Finally, the triangles are joined into rows to minimize the number of set-in seams. Color placement—both the colors and color values—is very important to the success of the quilt design, so planning the overall color layout first is absolutely necessary.

CHOOSING FABRICS

Choose as many fabrics as possible with light, medium, and dark color values. For more information about color value, see "What Is Color Value?" on page 106. In the quilt shown, each pinwheel is made from the same color family; for instance, all six spokes are medium blue, or all are kelly green; none of the six

spokes, however, are the exact same fabric. If you don't have quite as large a fabric collection as this quiltmaker did, try making all six spokes of a pinwheel from the same fabric. Your quilt will still have a scrappy feel, but you won't need to collect quite as many fabrics.

Rows of pinwheels alternate between light and dark, but the lights are very light and the darks

Quilt Size	
Finished Quilt Size	83" × 97"
Number of Pieced Triangles	434
Finished Triangle Size	approximately 4½" per side

NOTE: Due to the complexity of the design, no size variations are given.

Materials	
	Amount
Assorted light prints	1⅓ yards
Assorted medium prints	2½ yards
Assorted dark prints	3¾ yards
Black print	1⅞ yards
Medium print	1½ yards
Stripe	⅝ yard
Backing	7¾ yards
Batting	91" × 105"
Binding	¾ yard

NOTE: Yardages are based on 44/45-inch-wide fabrics that are at least 42 inches wide after preshrinking.

Cutting Chart			
Fabric	**Used For**	**Piece**	**Number to Cut**
Light prints	Patchwork	A	240
Medium prints	Patchwork	A	468
Dark prints	Patchwork	A	732
Black print	Outer quilt edges	A	42
	Outer quilt edges	B	45
	Outer quilt edges	C	34
	Outer quilt edges	D	29
	Outer quilt edges	E	15
Fabric	**Used For**	**Strip Width**	**Number to Cut**
Black print	First border	2½"	7
	Last border	2¼"	7
Stripe	Second border	1¼"	7
	Fourth border	1¼"	7
Medium print	Third border	7"	7

are really medium hues in the top left corner. In the opposite corner, the darks are very dark, with lots of black prints, and the lights are medium tones.

With the exception of black, all of the other prints in this quilt are cool colors. For a different look, use a fall color palette, or try a monochromatic design with hundreds of blue fabrics, for example, ranging from the palest opal to deep indigo.

Photocopy the **Color Plan** on page 93, and use crayons or colored pencils to develop a color scheme that suits you and your scrap bag.

CUTTING

Construct durable templates of pattern pieces A, B, C, D, and E on pages 91–92, as these templates will be used to cut many pieces. It is helpful to mark the seam line on the back of the A, B, and D pieces, so you'll have guidelines for set-in seams. Window templates will work well for this purpose; see page 110 for more information.

All measurements include ¼-inch seam allowances. Refer to the Cutting Chart to cut the required number of pieces from each fabric.

Note: Cut and piece together a few sample triangle units before cutting all the fabric for the quilt.

LAYING OUT THE QUILT

Step 1. Use a design wall or other flat surface to arrange all of the A pieces in this quilt. If you don't

— Sew Easy —

If you plan to hand piece this quilt, transfer the midpoint mark on the longest side of the A pattern piece onto your fabric pieces. It will help you match your pieces as you stitch them together. If you are machine piecing, this mark is not as crucial, yet it can help you align your quilt rows. When the midpoint of A in one row is aligned with the seam between two A pieces in the adjacent row, the result will be perfect patchwork!

have a wall large enough to accommodate the entire layout, arrange the pieces on a sheet or blanket placed on the floor. As you arrange your pieces, be sure you form pinwheels of the same color and value where the sides of the trapezoids meet, as shown in **Diagram 1**.

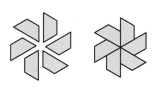

Diagram 1

Step 2. Although there are a few exceptions, both color and value change from row to row diagonally across the top of the quilt, beginning with one light pinwheel in the upper left corner. Next, lay out a row of three medium dark pinwheels, followed by a row of five very light pinwheels. The blades of adjacent pinwheels fit into each other, as shown in **Diagram 2**.

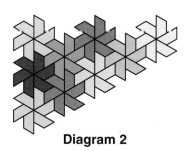

Diagram 2

Step 3. Most of the darkest rows contain only dark pinwheels, while most of the lighter rows contain pinwheels of varying color value from very light to medium light. Referring to the photograph on page 84, continue laying out rows of pinwheels, alternating from light to dark. Notice that the values get darker as you add more diagonal rows. In the middle rows, there is not as much contrast between the light and dark values. As you near the bottom right corner, the darks are very dark, and the light rows are medium shades. When you have laid out all of the A pieces, the outer edges of your quilt will be jagged, as shown in **Diagram 2**. When the initial layout is complete,

step back and take a look at your quilt, and move the A pieces around until you are satisfied with the look.

Step 4. Fill in the jagged, outer edges with the black print A, B, C, D, and E pieces, as shown in **Diagram 3**.

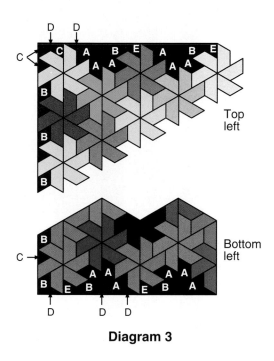

Diagram 3

Piecing the Quilt Top

The pinwheels are laid out in diagonal rows across the quilt top, but the actual piecing is done in vertical rows. First, the A pieces are sewn together in groups of three to form equilateral triangles. Then the triangles are stitched together in rows, as shown in the **Assembly Diagram** on page 88.

Piecing the Triangle Units

Step 1. Look at Row 2 in the **Assembly Diagram**. Work with three A pieces at a time from your layout, sewing them into equilateral triangles.

Align two A pieces, as shown in **Diagram 4A** on page 88, with right sides together. Begin stitching at the edge that will be the outer edge of the triangle. End the seam ¼ inch from the opposite

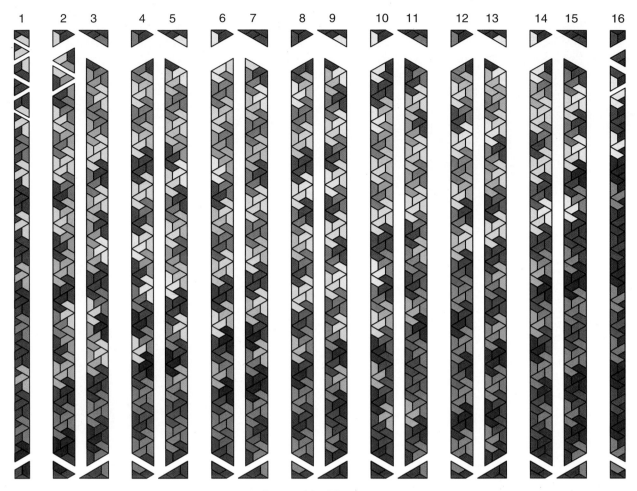

Assembly Diagram

edge (or at the intersection of seam lines if you marked the reverse of each piece), and backstitch. For more information about set-in seams, see page 108. Open out the top piece and press as desired.

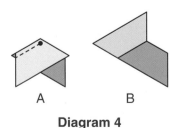

A   B

Diagram 4

Step 2. With right sides together, align the third A piece with the partially assembled unit, as shown in **Diagram 5A.** Begin stitching at the outer edge of the triangle unit; stop when you get

to the pivot point and backstitch. Reposition the pieces (see **5B**), and finish sewing the third A piece to the unit, beginning where the last seam ended. Press all seams flat, as shown in **5C.**

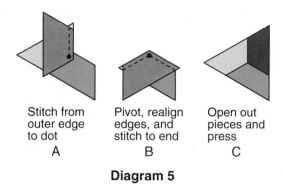

Stitch from outer edge to dot
A

Pivot, realign edges, and stitch to end
B

Open out pieces and press
C

Diagram 5

Step 3. Put the completed triangle in your quilt layout, positioning colors correctly. Repeat until all triangles are pieced.

PIECING THE PARTIAL TRIANGLES

The units in the outer rows of the quilt, as well as those at the top and bottom of each inner row, are assembled in a similar manner, but they use a combination of A, B, C, D, and E pieces, all cut from the black print. As you piece each unit, re-place it in the quilt layout, checking for correct color placement, before continuing on to the next.

Top Units

Step 1. Two types of units are used along the top of the quilt. The vertical rows in the **Assembly Diagram** are shown in pairs. For the top unit of the left row, sew D to A, as shown in **Diagram 6A,** ending ¼ inch from the edge of the pieces. Set in the remaining A piece as before. See **6B.** Press the seams flat. Repeat, making a total of seven units.

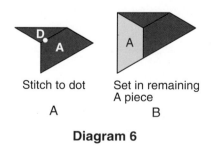

Stitch to dot
A

Set in remaining A piece
B

Diagram 6

Step 2. For the top right unit of each pair, sew D, B, and A pieces together, as shown in **Diagram 7A.**

Then sew E to the unit, as shown in **7B.** Press the seams flat. Make a total of seven units.

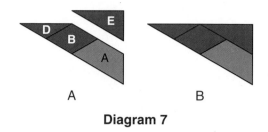

A

B

Diagram 7

Bottom Units

Step 1. Two types of units are also used along the bottom of the quilt. For the left row, sew A to B, as shown in **Diagram 8A.** Then sew E to the unit, as shown in **8B.** Press the seams flat. Repeat, making a total of seven units.

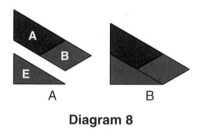

A

B

Diagram 8

Step 2. The bottom right unit is made of two A and two D pieces sewn together, as shown in **Diagram 9A.** Sew the units together, pivoting and setting in the seams, as shown in **9B.** Press the seams flat. Make a total of seven units.

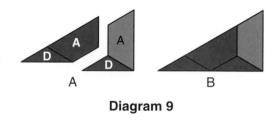

A

B

Diagram 9

Side Units

Step 1. Two types of side units are used in the outer vertical rows of the quilt. For the first unit in each row, sew an A to a C, as shown in **Diagram 10** on page 90. Press the seam. Make 33 side units.

Diagram 10

Step 2. For the second side unit, stitch two A pieces together, as shown in **Diagram 11A**, stopping ¼ inch from the edge where a B piece will be set in. Backstitch. Set in B, as shown in **11B**. Press the seams flat. Make a total of 30 side units.

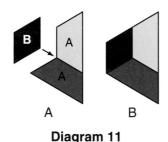

Diagram 11

Corners

Step 1. To complete the upper left corner, stitch a single E triangle to the first side unit in the row.

Step 2. Piece the upper right and lower left corners, as shown in **Diagram 12**. Sew D to A, as shown, then set in B as before. Press the seams flat.

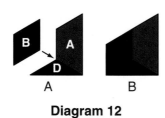

Diagram 12

Step 3. For the lower right corner, sew C to A, as shown in **Diagram 13A**. Then sew E to the unit, as shown in **13B**. Press the seams.

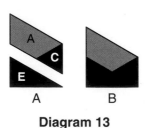

Diagram 13

SEWING THE ROWS TOGETHER

Step 1. Referring again to the **Assembly Diagram** on page 88, sew the units in the outer vertical rows together, including the corner pieces.

Step 2. Sew together all of the Row 2 triangles. Then attach the top and bottom units. Sew the Row 3 triangles together, leaving off the end units. Pin the partially completed Row 3 to Row 2, aligning it so the seams meet to form the first full pinwheel. See **Diagram 14**. Pin at each seam intersection, then stitch the rows together. Finish the wide row by attaching the remaining top unit, as shown. Attach the bottom unit in a similar manner. Repeat with all row pairs.

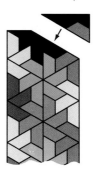

Diagram 14

Step 3. Sew all rows together to complete the quilt top, carefully matching the seams where pinwheels meet. Press the quilt.

ADDING THE MITERED BORDERS

This quilt has five borders, as shown in the **Quilt Diagram** on page 92. Sew the strips for each side together first, then add them to the quilt top as a single unit, mitering the corners.

Step 1. To determine the correct length for the side borders, measure the quilt top vertically through the center. To this measurement, add two times the finished width of all five borders (11¾ inches × 2 = 23½ inches), plus 5 inches. This is the length you will need to make all side border strips. In the same manner, measure the quilt top horizontally through the center to calculate the length of the top and bottom borders. Sew like border strips together end to end until you've achieved the required lengths for each border.

Step 2. Pin and sew the five side border strips together lengthwise into two units, as shown in **Diagram 15.** Press all seams toward the outer border. Assemble the top and bottom borders in the same manner. Press seams toward the inner border.

Diagram 15

Step 3. Center, pin, and sew the four border units to the quilt top, making sure the wider black print border is aligned with the quilt edges. Refer to page 119 for finishing the mitered border corners. Be sure to match like strips in adjacent borders.

QUILTING AND FINISHING

Step 1. Mark the quilt top for quilting. The pinwheels in the quilt shown were outline quilted.

Straight vertical lines were quilted in the narrow inner and outer borders, and diagonal lines were quilted in the wide inner border.

Step 2. To make the quilt backing, cut the backing fabric crosswise into three equal pieces, and trim the selvages. Cut a 32-inch-wide segment from two of the pieces, then sew a narrow segment to each side of the full-width piece, as shown in **Diagram 16.** Press the seams open.

Diagram 16

Step 3. Layer the quilt top, batting, and backing, and baste. Quilt as desired.

Step 4. Referring to page 121, make and attach double-fold binding. To calculate the amount of binding needed for your quilt, add the length of the four sides of the quilt plus 9 inches.

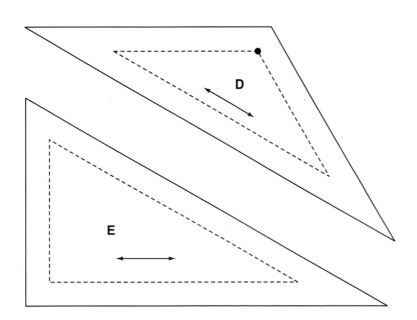

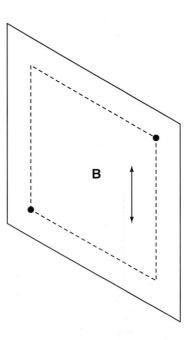

Quilt Diagram

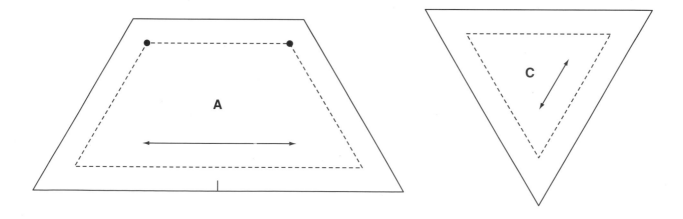

Evening at the Lily Pond
Color Plan

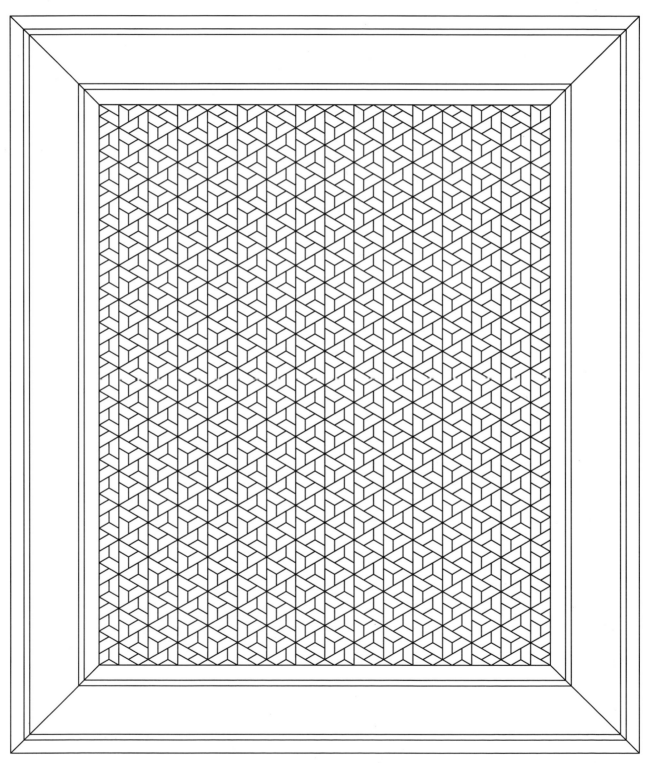

Photocopy this page and use it to experiment with color schemes for your quilt.

TUMBLING BLOCKS

Skill Level: *Intermediate*

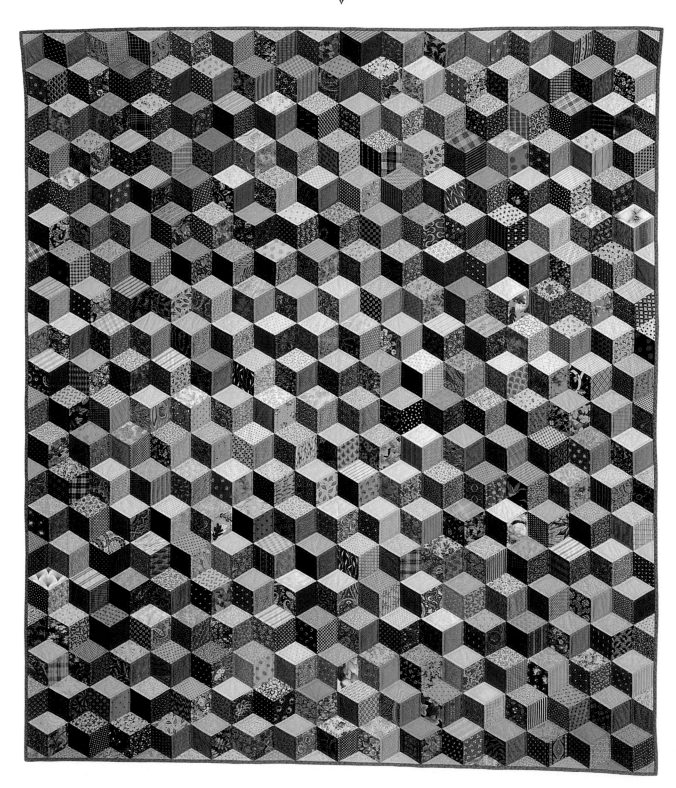

*T*umbling Blocks is an old-time favorite One Patch pattern that was often pieced as a charm quilt from hundreds of different fabrics. Charm quilt folklore says that while it is the intention for each fabric to be used only once, there is always at least one fabric repeated in the quilt. Sure enough, quiltmaker Jacqueline Chace's young daughter discovered that one or two fabrics were accidentally repeated, making this twin-size quilt a true replica of a vintage charm quilt. Earthy colors typical of the 1800s and no border also add to the old-fashioned feel of this beauty.

BEFORE YOU BEGIN

The instructions are for machine piecing this Tumbling Blocks quilt. If you need more information for piecing set-in seams, be sure to read page 108. If you prefer hand piecing, refer to the directions for Damon's Diamond Delight on page 36, which is a Tumbling Blocks variation that is English paper pieced.

CHOOSING FABRICS

This charm quilt contains 60 degree diamonds, which are cut from hundreds of scraps of dark, medium, and light fabrics. Placement of color value is consistent in each Tumbling Block, but notice that all light fabrics used are not of the same value, nor are all mediums or all darks the same. Even though our instructions refer to fabric placement by only those three terms, don't feel you must match all fabrics in each group to obtain three exact values. The perceived value

Quilt Sizes

	Crib	Twin (shown)
Finished Quilt Size	40½" × 54½"	75½" × 90½"

Materials

	Crib	Twin
Assorted light prints	1⅜ yards	3¾ yards
Assorted medium prints	1¼ yards	3½ yards
Assorted dark prints	1¼ yards	3½ yards
Backing	3½ yards	5½ yards
Batting	48" × 60"	84" × 98"
Binding	⅜ yard	¾ yard
Paper for piecing (optional)		

NOTE: Yardages are based on 44/45-inch-wide fabrics that are at least 42 inches wide after preshrinking.

of a fabric is determined by the fabrics that surround it, which allows you more freedom in your selections. For more details on color value, see page 106.

The fabrics used in this quilt are all prints. Some are so subtle that they appear to be solids from a distance, yet they provide more texture than solids and help add visual interest to a quilt.

If you don't have a fabric or scrap collection large enough to cut all of your diamonds from different fabrics, try swapping with friends or scouting your

Cutting Chart

Fabric	Used For	Piece	Number to Cut	
			Crib	Twin
Light prints	Hexagon units	A	83	276
	Side units	B	10	18
	Top and bottom units	C	14	28
	Corner units	D and D reverse	2	2
Medium prints	Hexagon units	A	96	300
Dark prints	Hexagon units	A	96	300

NOTE: *The number of pieces to cut is the total needed to complete the quilt. You may want to cut extra of each so you will have color options when assembling your quilt.*

local fabric shops for sale fabrics or inexpensive fat eighths and fat quarters. Or simply limit the number of fabrics by repeating them several times each. Your quilt will have a scrappy effect as long as you have about 30 or so fabrics each of light, medium, and dark values.

If you'd like to create a different color scheme, photocopy the **Color Plan** on page 103, and use crayons or colored pencils to plan your own color arrangement.

CUTTING

Construct durable templates of pattern pieces A, B, C, and D on pages 101–102. We recommend that you make window templates, which will enable you to mark the cutting line and seam line with the same template. For more information about constructing window templates, see page 110. Be sure to mark the pivot points (the dots at each seam intersection) on the reverse side of each piece when you cut it out. Knowing where the seam intersections are will make it much easier to match pieces and set in seams when you sew pieces together. Or see the "Sew Easy" box for another way to know where to start and stop your seams.

If you are using fabric with a directional pattern, align the fabric pattern with the grain arrow on the pattern pieces. After cutting your fabric, group the pieces by dark, medium, or light value.

If you will be using the English paper piecing method, cut out paper pieces on the inner, dashed line of the patterns, which indicates the finished size of the piece. You will need one paper template for each fabric piece.

All measurements include ¼-inch seam allowances. Refer to the Cutting Chart for the types and number of pieces you need to cut from each template.

Note: Cut and piece one sample hexagon unit before cutting all the fabric for the quilt.

PIECING THE QUILT TOP

The diamonds are pieced together into multi-diamond units shaped like a hexagon. These hexagon units are then pieced together to form the quilt top. Variations of the basic pieced hexagon unit are used around the top, bottom, and side edges of the quilt.

The following list shows how many of each type of unit to make:

Unit	Number for Crib	Number for Twin
Hexagon	14	56
Side	4	8
Corner	2	2
Top	3	7
Bottom	4	7

Hexagon Units

Step 1. On a flat surface, arrange four dark A diamonds, four medium A diamonds, and four light A diamonds into the multidiamond hexagon-shaped unit, as shown in **Diagram 1**. Rearrange the diamonds until you've achieved a desirable layout, swapping selected pieces with others from the stack of the same color value, if necessary.

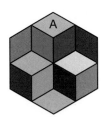

Diagram 1

Step 2. Sew together the four pairs of medium and dark diamonds, as shown in **Diagram 2**. End seams at the pivot points and backstitch slightly.

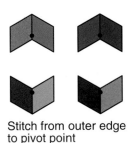

Stitch from outer edge
to pivot point

Diagram 2

Step 3. Sew a light diamond to two of the pairs, pivoting and setting in the seams where indicated in **Diagram 3**. Sew the remaining two diamond pairs to the cubes you just formed, as shown, pivoting again to set in the light diamonds. For more information on setting in seams, read the instructions on page 108.

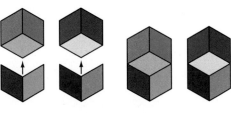

Diagram 3

Sew Easy

If you don't want to take the time to mark pivot points at the corners of all of your diamonds, try this handy masking tape idea. Mark the pivot point on your first pair of diamonds to be sewn together. With their right sides together, place them under your machine's presser foot. Insert the needle exactly through the pivot point. With the needle down, align the right edges of your diamonds with the seam guide (or the presser foot if it's exactly ¼ inch wide). Once you have your diamonds lined up, place a piece of masking tape along the back, angled edge of your layered diamonds. This will be your alignment guide for all subsequent pairs of diamonds. If you prefer, you can use several layers of tape to make a firmer edge against which you can align your fabric.

Now you're ready to sew. Begin stitching, backstitch, and then stitch to the pivot point at the other end of the diamonds. Stop stitching, but leave the needle down in the fabric. Place another piece of masking tape along the diagonal edge of the front of the diamond in the same manner as you did in the back. Layer the tape if you wish. Once the tape is in place, continue stitching to the end of the fabric. This front marking will be used later when you begin setting in other diamonds.

Step 4. Referring to **Diagram 4**, sew two light diamonds to one of the units completed in Step 3. End each seam at the pivot point and backstitch.

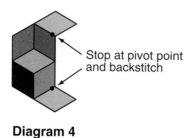

Stop at pivot point and backstitch

Diagram 4

Step 5. Referring to **Diagram 5**, add the remaining unit from Step 3, stitching in the direction of the arrows and pivoting twice to set in the seam.

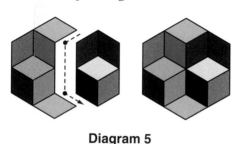

Diagram 5

Step 6. Repeat Steps 1 through 5 to assemble the number of hexagon units required for your quilt size.

Side and Corner Units

Step 1. Using two dark A diamonds, two medium A diamonds, and one light A diamond, assemble the unit in **Diagram 6A** in the same manner as you pieced the larger, hexagon-shaped units.

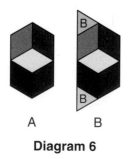

A   B

Diagram 6

Step 2. Sew a light B triangle to the top left and bottom left of the unit, as shown in **6B**. Repeat,

making the number of side units required for your quilt size.

Step 3. For the corner units, assemble two units shown in **6A**. Then attach one light B triangle and one light D or D reverse corner triangle, as dictated by the size quilt you are making. See **Diagram 7**. (Remember that you will only need two of these corner units per quilt.)

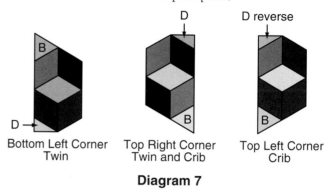

Bottom Left Corner Twin

Top Right Corner Twin and Crib

Top Left Corner Crib

Diagram 7

Top and Bottom Units

The units used along the top and bottom edges of the quilt are assembled in the same manner as the basic hexagon unit, but with the variation shown in **Diagram 8**. For the top units, the light diamond on the top edge of the unit is replaced by a light C triangle. For the bottom units, the bottom light diamond is replaced by a light C triangle. Set in the triangles in the same manner as you set in the diamonds previously. Make the number of top and bottom units required for your quilt size.

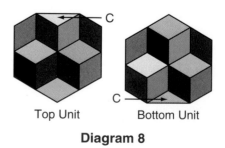

Top Unit

Bottom Unit

Diagram 8

ASSEMBLING THE QUILT TOP

Step 1. Use a design wall or other flat surface to arrange the quilt components into horizontal rows, as shown in the assembly diagrams on this page and page 100. Arrange the remaining light C triangles along the top and bottom edges of the quilt, as shown. Place D triangles in the corners. If necessary, move all components around until you are happy with the overall color placement.

Crib Assembly Diagram

Step 2. Sew each light C triangle in the top row to the unit directly to its left, as shown in **Diagram 9.** End your seam and backstitch at the pivot point. In the same manner, sew C triangles in the bottom row to the units directly to their right.

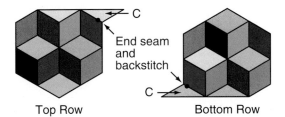

Diagram 9

Step 3. Sew the top row units together, starting at the outer edge of the C triangle and pivoting to set in the seams, as shown in **Diagram 10.** End each seam at the pivot point ¼ inch from the end

of the unit and backstitch. Hexagon units will be set in to these junctions when the rows are sewn together.

Diagram 10

Step 4. Sew the bottom row units together in the same manner as for the top row units.

Step 5. Sew the remaining hexagon units and side units together in horizontal rows, beginning and ending each seam at the pivot point, as shown in **Diagram 11.**

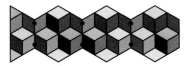

Diagram 11

Step 6. Sew the rows together, setting in the light diamonds where they meet the seams that connect the hexagon and side units, as shown in **Diagram 12.** Sew the light D and D reverse triangles to the corners of the quilt. Press the quilt top. See the **Quilt Diagram** on page 101.

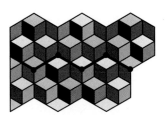

Diagram 12

Quilting and Finishing

Step 1. Mark the quilt top for quilting, if desired. In the quilt shown, each diamond was outline quilted ¼ inch from the seams.

D   C

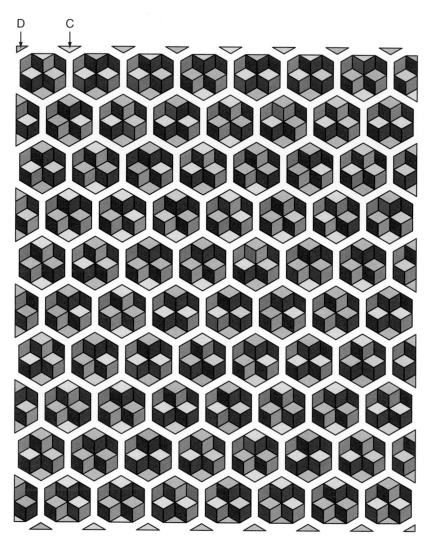

Twin-Size Assembly Diagram

Step 2. Regardless of which quilt size you have chosen to make, the backing will have to be pieced. For the crib quilt, cut the backing fabric in half crosswise, and trim the selvages. Cut two 16½-inch-wide panels from one piece and a third 16½-inch-wide segment from the remaining piece. Sew the three pieces together lengthwise, as shown in **Diagram 13**. Press the seams open.

Step 3. For the twin-size quilt, cut the backing fabric in half crosswise, and trim the selvages. Cut one piece in half lengthwise. Sew the half-width panels to either side of the full-width piece, as shown. Press the seams open.

Step 4. Layer the quilt top, batting, and backing, and baste. Quilt as desired.

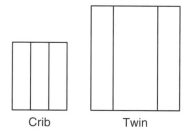

Crib   Twin

Diagram 13

Step 5. Referring to the directions on page 121, make and attach double-fold binding. To calculate the amount of binding needed, add the length of the four sides of the quilt plus 9 inches. The total is the approximate number of inches of binding you will need.

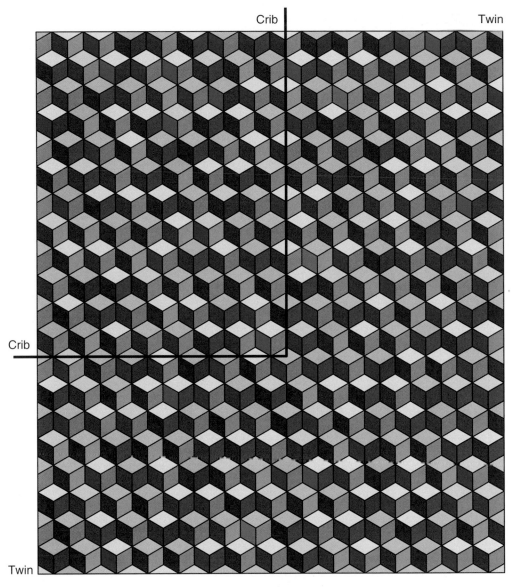

Crib

Twin

Crib

Twin

Quilt Diagram

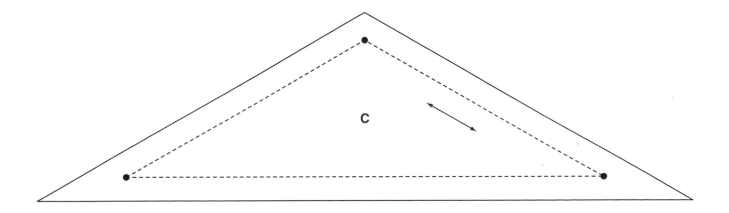

C

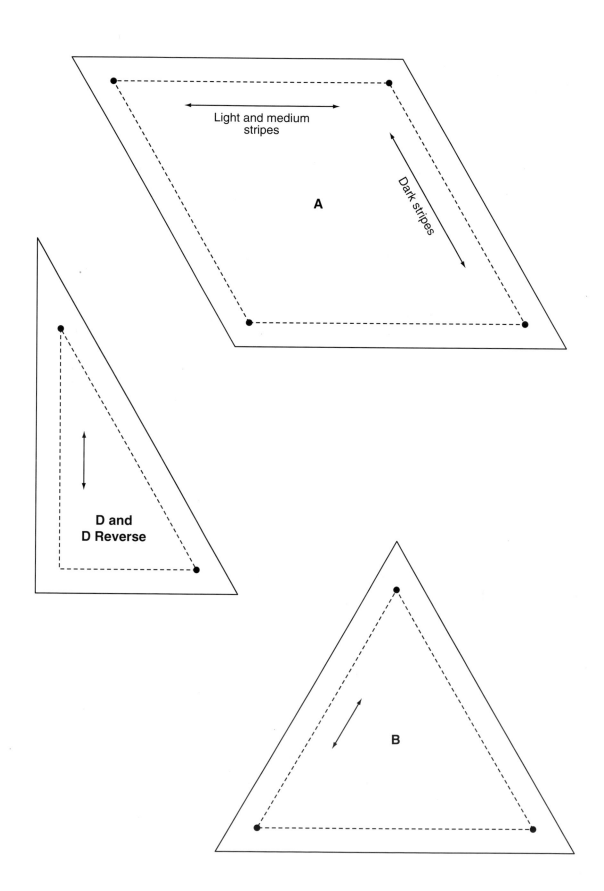

TUMBLING BLOCKS
Color Plan

Photocopy this page and use it to experiment with color schemes for your quilt.

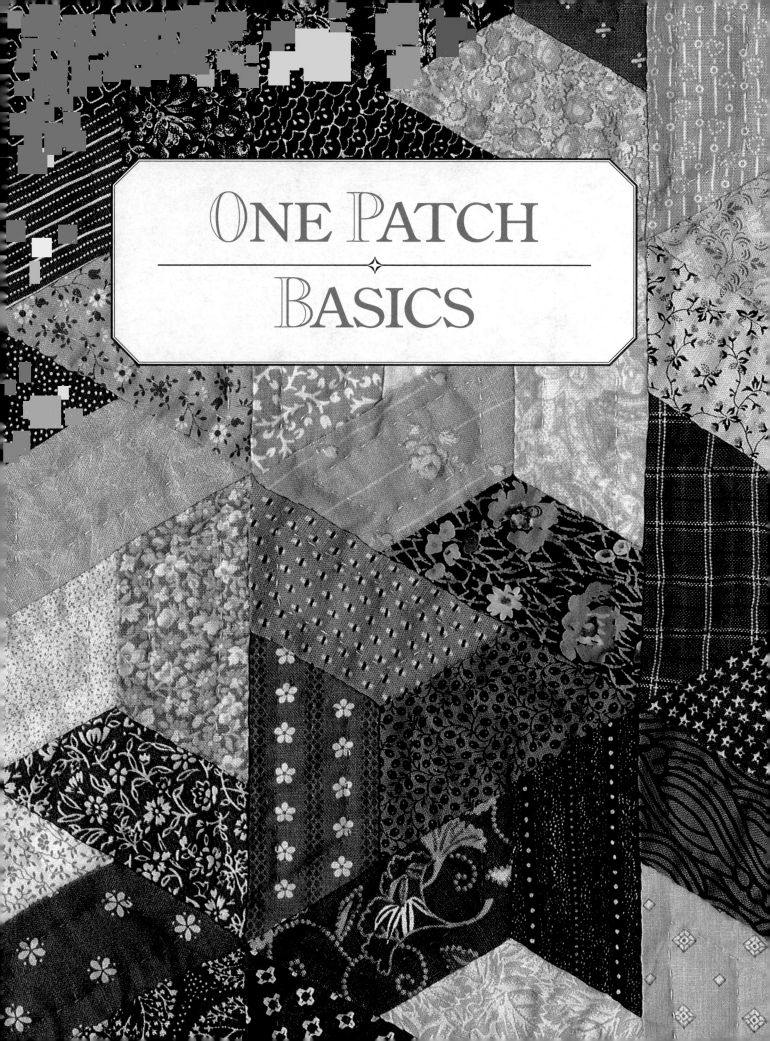

One Patch
Basics

USING ONE PATCH BASICS

Each project in this book contains detailed step-by-step directions to make the quilt shown. In this section, you'll find helpful information and tips pertaining to One Patch quilts in general, including ideas on working with color placement, scrap quilts, piecing techniques, and template options.

WHAT IS A ONE PATCH QUILT?

The term One Patch refers to any quilt that is assembled by repeating the same shape piece over and over again. Common One Patch shapes include 60 degree hexagons and diamonds, clamshells, and spools. Multiples of these One Patch shapes don't form a typical square block when fit together. Instead, a quilt with jagged outer edges is formed. You can finish a quilt by applying binding around its pointed or curved edges, such as the Grandmother's Flower Garden quilt on page 28 or the Charming Spools quilt on page 52. These are true One Patch quilts. On the other hand, some quilters use variations of the original piece to fill in the gaps around the edges so that borders or binding can be applied to straight edges. An example of this is Tumbling Blocks on page 94. To square the quilt sides, pieces that are one-half or one-quarter of the original diamond shape are placed around the outer edges of the quilt.

CHOOSING FABRICS

What Is Color Value?

Placement of color value may be the most important factor in the overall design of a One Patch quilt. Don't be intimidated by the concept of color value; just think of it as the amount of contrast between fabrics when they are placed side by side. In any quilt, contrast between the different elements is a big factor in determining the design we perceive. As an example of design created through contrast, three versions of the Tumbling Blocks quilt are shown in **Diagram 1.**

The diamonds are positioned the same way in all three quilts, but the altered placement of color value gives each a totally different appearance.

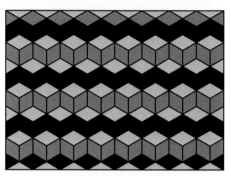

Diagram 1

The directions for each project include recommendations for value placement, usually referred to as dark, medium, and light. Those designations aren't meant to dictate that all darks be black or navy or that all lights be pale pastels. The starting point for value is up to you, and you may choose to alter the overall appearance of the quilt by changing the intensity of all of the values in general or by changing the number of pieces cut from specific values.

As you design a quilt, keep in mind that the perceived value of a fabric depends on the fabric it is positioned next to. For example, a medium blue fabric looks dark when positioned against a pastel, but it can become a light or medium when positioned next to black, as shown in **Diagram 2.**

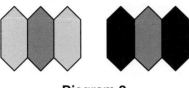

Diagram 2

To group fabrics by value, begin with a quick sort, stacking fabrics in piles according to your first impression of their value. Then go back and take a closer look at the contents of each pile. Place the fabrics side by side and view the entire group as a whole. If any fabric is noticeably lighter or darker than others in the group, such as the second fabric from the left in **Diagram 3**, remove it and consider using it with another group. Add and subtract fabrics until you have a good assortment for that particular value. Repeat the process for the remaining value groups.

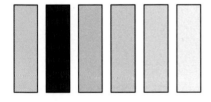

Diagram 3

As you work with color value, try to achieve a visible contrast between different value ranges (dark, medium, and light) and little to no contrast among fabrics in the same value range.

While sorting fabrics, you may find that color often incorrectly influences your perception of value. Here are several ways to solve this problem.

• View your fabrics through a special value filter that can help you sort them into light-to-dark gradations. These inexpensive red plastic filters mask color, making objects appear to the eye in shades of gray to black. The effect is similar to that of a black-and-white photograph. (Red usually appears lighter than it really is through these filters, so be sure to evaluate reds in other ways, too.)

• View the fabrics from a distance. Do they all blend together, or do a few still pop out at you?

• Glue or pin swatches of fabrics side by side on a piece of paper, and make a black-and-white photocopy of it.

Sew Easy

Visual texture is an important consideration when selecting fabrics. Try to choose fabrics of varying print scales and types, such as florals, geometrics, plaids, and pictorials to vary the visual texture as much as possible. Some prints are very big and bold. Others "read" as solids. These are fabrics that from a distance may appear solid, but a closer look shows that they are truly prints. This type of print provides a good transition when placed between bolder prints.

What Is a Scrap Quilt?

Most of the projects in this book are scrap quilts, which in the past meant exactly what the name implies—that they were assembled with scraps left over from other sewing projects, as well as remnants of worn-out clothing. Today, quilting is so popular that quilters often accumulate large collections of fabrics specifically for making scrap quilts. The repetitive nature of One Patch designs gives quiltmakers the opportunity to showcase their fabric collections and exhibit their skills in making those fabrics work together.

A One Patch design is also the perfect choice for a charm quilt—one in which no fabric is used more than once. Several of the quilts in this collection are charm quilts, including Natural Balance on page 2.

What if you don't have a large collection of fabric to select from? Here are several suggestions to supplement a beginning fabric collection.

• Buy packages of precut fabric squares. They are available from quilt shops and mail-order sources in a range of colors, styles, and sizes.

• If you attend quilt shows, seek out vendors who sell fat eighths and fat quarters of fabric. Unless you are strip piecing blocks, these wider pieces are often more useful than long, narrow ⅛- or ¼-yard cuts.

• Trade fabrics with friends. If you belong to a quilt guild, organize a fabric swap among members—cut all those fat quarters you picked up at the last quilt show in half, and trade to increase the variety of your collection.

• Do you own a computer and modem? If so, join one of the many on-line guilds. The ongoing fabric exchanges will keep your mailbox filled with a rainbow of fabrics from around the country.

── Sew Easy

A trick charm quilters use to expand their number of fabrics is to use the reverse side of a fabric to change its appearance. That way, the same fabric can be used twice in the quilt without breaking the no-repeat rule.

DESIGNING A ONE PATCH QUILT

When making a quilt with traditional, pieced blocks, the blocks are usually assembled first, arranged into a pleasing design, then sewn together to complete the quilt top. Some One Patch quilts can be made in the same manner, but often the design is established by arranging single pieces rather than multipiece blocks. Once the quilt layout is complete, the pieces are joined into larger units or directly into rows.

For the scrap projects in this book, it is best to cut extra pieces in each value range. You'll find that the additional fabric you use and the time spent cutting it will be worthwhile when the design process begins. The more pieces you have to choose from, the easier it will be to lay out the quilt in a pleasing color arrangement.

── Sew Easy

Fat quarters and fat eighths are normally cut as shown here. These cuts are popular with quilters, since the additional width gained by cutting the fabric this way is more useful for many projects than narrow, standard yardage cuts.

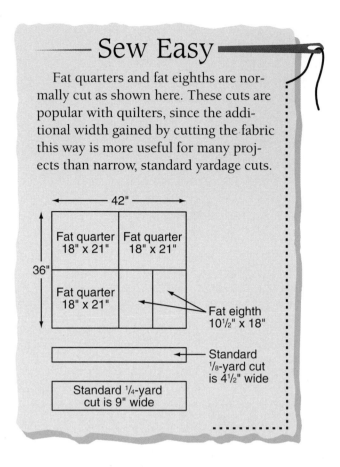

SEWING A ONE PATCH QUILT

Set-In Seams

Because many One Patch quilts contain irregularly shaped pieces, set-in seams are common. Refer to page 117 for additional instructions about setting in pieces. That section also contains general instructions for hand piecing and for using templates when hand piecing set-in seams.

Note, however, that the pattern pieces in this book contain black dots at seam line intersections when the pieces will need to be set in. Project directions refer to these markings as pivot points. You will be instructed to stitch the seam to the pivot point (rather than to the end of the fabric). You will then be instructed to either backstitch or pivot and continue stitching along the next seam line. Individual project directions will guide you through the assembly process, but be sure to mark the pivot points on your templates and on your fabric pieces.

The following steps explain the basics of English paper piecing, using a hexagon as an example. The basic steps are the same for all types of pieces.

Step 1. Center a paper piece on the back side of a fabric piece and pin it in place. Fold the seam allowance over the paper piece one side at a time and press. Baste the seam allowance to the paper, making sure you secure areas where the seam allowance overlaps. See **Diagram 4.** Repeat the steps with remaining pieces.

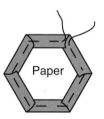

Diagram 4

Step 2. With right sides facing, place two hexagons together, matching edges carefully. Using a whipstitch, join edges together from corner to corner along one side, backstitching at the beginning and end of the seam. Take small stitches, and avoid sewing into the edges of the paper. Your stitches should barely show when the pieces are opened. See **Diagram 5.**

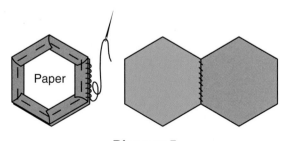

Diagram 5

Step 3. Sew the remaining pieces to the unit, as specified in the project directions. Sew each side from end to end in the same manner, matching edges carefully. It's not necessary to cut the thread at each corner; simply reposition the pieces so the next edges you want to sew are aligned and keep sewing. Even though you are not ending your

---

Sew Quick

Not every quilter wants to make the same size quilt, so size variations are included whenever possible. For some of the more complex designs, however, there simply isn't enough room to show two totally different quilt layouts and color schemes. However, if you'd like to alter the size of a quilt in this book, you can do so quickly and easily by simply changing the size of your template. For instance, if you love Charming Spools on page 52, but would rather make a wallhanging size for your sewing room, consider reducing the size of the pattern on a photocopier. Or, if you would like to make Damon's Diamond Delight on page 36 a bit larger without losing the large central diamond motif, start with a slightly larger diamond. Just remember, you'll need to adjust your yardage requirements accordingly.

English Paper Piecing

English paper piecing is a hand-piecing method that is useful for many One Patch quilts. This technique has traditionally been used for hexagons, such as the ones in Grandmother's Flower Garden (page 28), but it can be used with pieces of any shape. The fabric seam allowance is basted to paper templates that have been cut to the finished size of each piece, then edges of adjoining pieces are whipstitched together. Paper piecing does require more time than other methods, but if you like to hand sew, the precision it adds to a project makes the extra time worthwhile.

Many types of paper can be used for paper piecing. Card-stock paper works well, but some quilters prefer ordinary typing paper. Freezer paper is another possibility, and it eliminates seam basting. When planning the number of paper pieces you'll need, remember that they can be reused, but each is left in place until all neighboring pieces have been sewn to the piece it is basted to.

thread, it's helpful to backstitch at each end of each seam for strength. Papers should be left in place until all adjacent pieces are sewn to a hexagon.

For more information about the English paper piecing technique, refer to the project directions for Damon's Diamond Delight (page 36) or Grandmother's Flower Garden (page 28).

Window Templates

Window templates work well with the paper piecing method. The inside edge of the window is the finished size of the piece and is used to mark the paper templates. This line can also be used to mark the seam line directly on pieces that will be set in. The outside edge of the template is the size of the piece plus a ¼-inch seam allowance and is used to mark the cutting line on the fabric.

To make a window template, transfer all lines of the pattern piece in the book onto durable template plastic. Use a sharp blade to cut out the shape on both the inner, dashed seam line and outer, solid cutting line. It is important that the template material be sturdy, as it will be traced around many (even hundreds) times. Since a window template is only ¼ inch wide on all edges, cardboard won't hold up to repeated use.

·······Sew Quick·······

If you use window templates, you don't have to mark the pivot dots on your fabric pieces. By tracing around the inner lines of the window template, you are marking the seam lines and the points where they intersect. You don't have to make a dot, either. Just stop stitching or pivot where your pencil lines meet.

Binding One Patch Quilts

If you are making one of the quilts in this book with borders or straight edges, you can refer to page 121 for more information on making binding

·······Sew Quick·······

Using freezer paper for your foundation papers can speed up the process of preparing your fabric pieces for hand sewing. Cut the freezer paper pieces, then position them waxy side up on the wrong side of a fabric piece. Use a medium to hot, dry iron to press the seam allowances onto the paper. The waxy coating will soften and hold the fabric in place, and you won't have to hand baste each piece or remove the basting stitches when your quilt is assembled.

and finishing quilt edges. If, however, you are making one of the projects with irregular-shaped edges, such as Grandmother's Flower Garden (page 28) or Charming Spools (page 52), your quilt will need a special binding treatment. Note that it is best to hand sew the binding in these cases.

First calculate the amount of binding needed by measuring the length of one side of the hexagon, the length of the curve of the spool, or the side of whatever unusual shape you need to bind. Then multiply this measurement by the number of those sides, hexagon angles, or spool curves along the outside edges of your quilt. The total is the number of inches of binding you will need. Add 10 to 15 extra inches as a little insurance. Then follow these pointers for a perfectly finished edges.

Step 1. Make narrow single-fold bias binding (cut strips about 1 inch wide) in the length you just calculated. It will be easier to apply a narrow binding around all those angles or curves.

Step 2. Trim the batting and backing even with the edges of the quilt top, and, with right sides together, pin about 6 inches of the binding to the quilt at a time. With a single strand of thread, work from the top side of the quilt and sew a ¼-inch seam allowance through the binding and all three layers of the quilt. Use a running stitch and backstitch occasionally.

Step 3. For hexagons, pivot at each outer and inner corner, as shown in **Diagram 6**. For spools or clamshells, you will also need to pivot where the curves change from convex to concave, as shown in **Diagram 7**. Also, when stitching binding along the curves, be careful not to pull the bias binding too tight, or you will have rippled edges when you're finished.

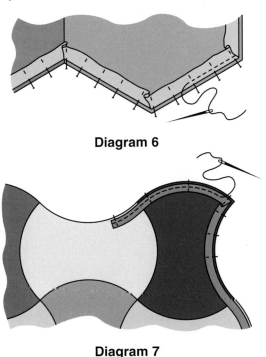

Diagram 6

Diagram 7

Step 4. Fold the binding to the back of the quilt and blindstitch it in place, forming tucks at each inner corner and slight miters at each outer point, as shown in **Diagram 8**.

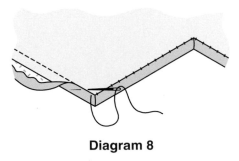

Diagram 8

FINISHING WITHOUT BINDING

Although it is possible to bind curved-edge quilts, such as Charming Spools on page 52, you

can also finish the edges without binding. The alternate finishing technique requires blindstitching by hand, but it offers a precise way to handle the curves of One Patch or even Wedding Ring quilts. You should note, however, that this type of edge finish wears more easily than binding, so you may want to use this technique on a quilt that won't receive hard use, such as the Grandmother's Flower Garden wallhanging on page 28.

Step 1. Quilt to within ⅝ inch of the quilt edges.

Step 2. Trim the batting so that it ends ¼ inch *inside* the edges of the quilt top. This will allow the batting to reach all the way to the quilt edges after you have finished sewing. Then trim the backing even with the edges of the quilt top.

Step 3. Turn under the ¼-inch seam allowances on both the quilt top and the backing, encasing the batting inside one of the seam allowances as you work, as shown in **Diagram 9**. Blindstitch all around the edges of the quilt.

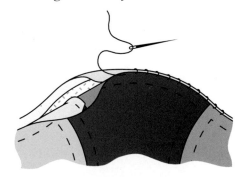

Diagram 9

Step 4. As a final touch, you may want to add quilting along the edges of the quilt to secure the batting in place, as shown in **Diagram 10**.

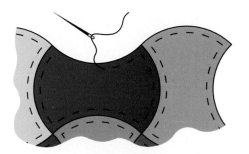

Diagram 10

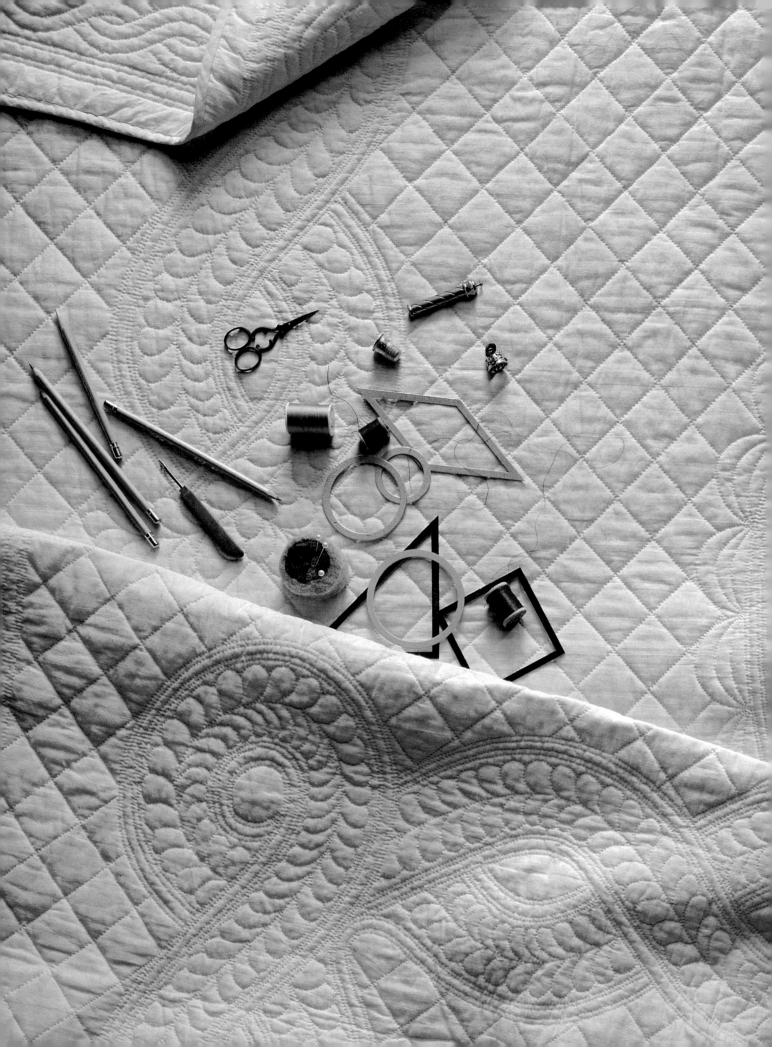

QUILTMAKING
BASICS

This section provides a refresher course in basic quiltmaking techniques. Refer to it as needed; it will help not only with the projects in this book but also with all your quiltmaking.

QUILTMAKER'S BASIC SUPPLY LIST

Here's a list of items you should have on hand before beginning a project.

• **Iron and ironing board:** Make sure these are set up near your sewing machine. Careful pressing leads to accurate piecing.

• **Needles:** The two types of needles commonly used by quilters are *betweens,* short needles used for hand quilting, and *sharps,* long, very thin needles used for appliqué and hand piecing. The thickness of hand-sewing needles decreases as their size designation increases. For instance, a size 12 needle is smaller than a size 10.

• **Rotary cutter, plastic ruler, and cutting mat:** Fabric can be cut quickly and accurately with rotary-cutting equipment. There are a variety of cutters available, all with slightly different handle styles and safety latches. Rigid, see-through acrylic rulers are used with rotary cutters. A 6 × 24-inch ruler is a good size; for the most versatility, be sure it has 45 and 60 degree angle markings. A 14-inch square ruler will also be helpful for making sure blocks are square. Always use a special mat with a rotary cutter. The mat protects the work surface and helps to grip the fabric. Purchase the largest mat practical for your sewing area. A good all-purpose size is 18 × 24 inches.

• **Safety pins:** These are generally used to baste quilts for machine quilting. Use rustproof nickel-plated brass safety pins, preferably in size #0.

• **Scissors:** You'll need several pairs of scissors—shears for cutting fabric, general scissors for cutting paper and template plastic, and small, sharp embroidery scissors for trimming threads.

• **Seam ripper:** A seam ripper with a small, extra-fine blade slips easily under any stitch length.

• **Sewing machine:** Any machine with a straight stitch is suitable for piecing quilt blocks. Follow the manufacturer's recommendations for cleaning and servicing your sewing machine.

• **Straight pins:** Choose long, thin pins with glass or plastic heads that are easy to see against fabric so that you don't forget to remove one.

• **Template material:** Sheets of clear and opaque template plastic can be purchased at most quilt or craft shops. Gridded plastic is also available and may help you to draw shapes more easily. Various weights of cardboard can also be used for templates, including common household items like cereal boxes, poster board, and manila file folders.

• **Thimbles:** For hand quilting, a thimble is almost essential. Look for one that fits the finger you use to push the needle. The thimble should be snug enough to stay put when you shake your hand. There should be a bit of space between the end of your finger and the inside of the thimble.

• **Thread:** For hand or machine piecing, 100 percent cotton thread is a traditional favorite. Cotton-covered polyester is also acceptable. For hand quilting, use 100 percent cotton quilting thread. For machine quilting, you may want to try clear nylon thread as the top thread, with cotton thread in the bobbin.

• **Tweezers:** Keep a pair of tweezers handy for removing bits of thread from ripped-out seams and for pulling away scraps of removable foundations. Regular cosmetic tweezers will work fine.

SELECTING AND PREPARING FABRICS

The traditional fabric choice for quilts is 100 percent cotton. It handles well, is easy to care for, presses easily, and frays less than synthetic blends.

The yardages in this book are generous estimates based on 44/45-inch-wide fabrics. It's a good idea to always purchase a bit more fabric than necessary to compensate for shrinkage and occasional cutting errors.

Prewash your fabrics using warm water and a mild soap or detergent. Test for colorfastness by first soaking a scrap in warm water. If colors bleed, set the dye by soaking the whole piece of fabric in a solution of 3 parts cold water to 1 part vinegar. Rinse the fabric several times in warm water. If it still bleeds, don't use it in a quilt that will need laundering—save it for a wallhanging that won't get a lot of use.

After washing, preshrink your fabric by drying it in a dryer on the medium setting. To keep wrinkles under control, remove the fabric from the dryer while it's still slightly damp and press it immediately with a hot iron.

CUTTING FABRIC

The cutting instructions for each project follow the list of materials. Whenever possible, the instructions are written to take advantage of quick rotary-cutting techniques. In addition, some projects include patterns for those who prefer to make templates and scissor cut individual pieces.

Although rotary cutting can be faster and more accurate than cutting with scissors, it has one disadvantage: It does not always result in the most efficient use of fabric. In some cases, the method results in long strips of leftover fabric. Don't think of these as waste; just add them to your scrap bag for future projects.

Rotary-Cutting Basics

Follow these two safety rules every time you use a rotary cutter: Always cut *away* from yourself, and always slide the blade guard into place as soon as you stop cutting.

Step 1: You can cut several layers of fabric at a time with a rotary cutter. Fold the fabric with the selvage edges together. You can fold it again if you want, doubling the number of layers to be cut.

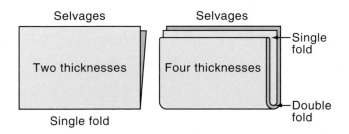

Step 2: To square up the end of the fabric, place a ruled square on the fold and slide a 6 × 24-inch ruler against the side of the square. Hold the ruler in place, remove the square, and cut along the edge of the ruler. If you are left-handed, work from the other end of the fabric.

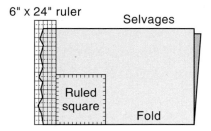

Step 3: For patchwork, cut strips or rectangles on the crosswise grain, then subcut them into smaller pieces as needed. The diagram shows a strip cut into squares.

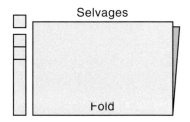

Step 4: A square can be subcut into two triangles by making one diagonal cut (A). Two diagonal cuts yield four triangles (B).

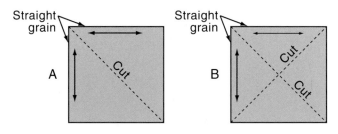

Step 5: Check strips periodically to make sure they're straight and not angled. If they are angled, refold the fabric and square up the edges again.

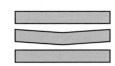

ENLARGING PATTERNS

Every effort has been made to provide full-size pattern pieces. But in some cases, where the pattern piece is too large to fit on the page, only one-half or one-quarter of the pattern is given. Instructions on the pattern piece will tell you where to position the pattern to continue tracing to make a full-size template.

MAKING AND USING TEMPLATES

To make a plastic template, place template plastic over the book page, trace the pattern onto the plastic, and cut out the template. To make a cardboard template, copy the pattern onto tracing paper, glue the paper to the cardboard, and cut out the template. With a permanent marker, record on every template any identification letters and grain lines, as well as the size and name of the block and the number of pieces needed. Always check your templates against the printed pattern for accuracy.

The patchwork patterns in this book are printed with double lines. The inner dashed line is the finished size of the piece, while the outer solid line includes seam allowance.

For hand piecing: Trace the inner line to make finished-size templates. Cut out the templates on the traced line. Draw around the templates on the wrong side of the fabric, leaving ½ inch between pieces. Then mark ¼-inch seam allowances before you cut out the pieces.

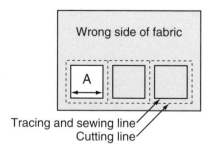

Wrong side of fabric

A

Tracing and sewing line
Cutting line

For machine piecing: Trace the outer solid line on the printed pattern to make templates with seam allowance included. Draw around the templates on the wrong side of the fabric and cut out the pieces on this line.

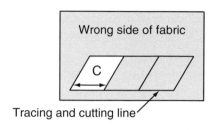

Wrong side of fabric

C

Tracing and cutting line

For appliqué: Appliqué patterns in this book have only a single line and are finished size. Draw around the templates on the right side of the fabric, leaving ½ inch between pieces. Add ⅛- to ¼-inch seam allowances by eye as you cut the pieces.

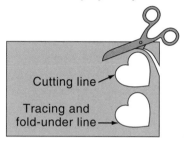

Cutting line

Tracing and
fold-under line

PIECING BASICS

Standard seam allowance for piecing is ¼ inch. Machine sew a sample seam to test the accuracy of the seam allowance; adjust as needed. For hand piecing, the sewing line is marked on the fabric.

Hand Piecing

Cut fabric pieces using finished-size templates. Place the pieces right sides together, match marked seam lines, and pin. Use a running stitch along the marked line, backstitching every four or five stitches and at the beginning and end of the seam.

When you cross seam allowances of previously joined units, leave the seam allowances free. Backstitch just before you cross, slip the needle through the seam allowance, backstitch just after you cross, then resume stitching the seam.

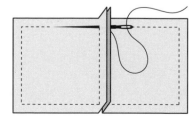

Machine Piecing

Cut the fabric pieces using templates with seam allowances included or using a rotary cutter and ruler without templates. Set the stitch length at 10 to 12 stitches per inch.

Place the fabric pieces right sides together, then sew from raw edge to raw edge. Press seams before crossing them with other seams, pressing toward the darker fabric whenever possible.

Chain piecing: Use this technique when you need to sew more than one of the same type of unit. Place the fabric pieces right sides together and, without lifting the presser foot or cutting the thread, run the pairs through the sewing machine one after another. Once all the units you need have been sewn, snip them apart and press.

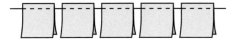

Setting In Pieces

Pattern pieces must sometimes be set into angles created by other pieces, as shown in the diagram. Here, pieces A, B, and C are set into the angles created by the four joined diamond pieces.

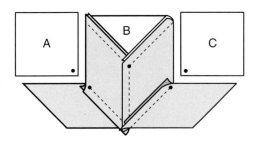

Step 1: Keep the seam allowances open where the piece is to be set in. Begin by sewing the first seam in the usual manner, beginning and ending the seam ¼ inch from the edge of the fabric and backstitching at each end.

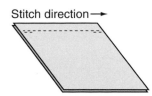

Stitch direction →

Step 2: Open up the pattern pieces and place the piece to be set in right sides together with one of the first two pieces. Begin the seam ¼ inch from the edge of the fabric and sew to the exact point where the first seam ended, backstitching at the beginning and end of the seam.

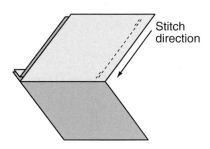

Stitch direction

Step 3: Rotate the pattern pieces so that you are ready to sew the final seam. Keeping the seam allowances free, sew from the point where the last seam ended to ¼ inch from the edge of the piece.

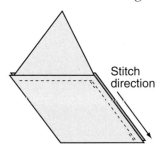

Stitch direction

Step 4: Press the seams so that as many of them as possible lie flat. The finished unit should look like the one shown here.

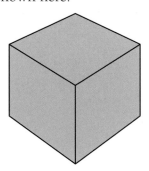

APPLIQUÉ BASICS

Review "Making and Using Templates" to learn how to prepare templates for appliqué. Lightly draw around each template on the right side of the fabric using a pencil or other nonpermanent marker. These are the fold-under lines. Cut out the pieces ⅛ to ¼ inch to the outside of the marked lines.

The Needle-Turn Method

Pin the pieces in position on the background fabric, always working in order from the background to the foreground. For best results, don't turn under or appliqué edges that will be covered by other appliqué pieces. Use a thread color that matches the fabric of the appliqué piece.

Step 1: Bring the needle up from under the appliqué patch exactly on the drawn line. Fold under the seam allowance on the line to neatly encase the knot.

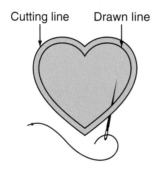

Cutting line   Drawn line

Step 2: Insert the tip of the needle into the background fabric right next to where the thread comes out of the appliqué piece. Bring the needle out of the background fabric approximately 1⁄16 inch away from and up through the very edge of the fold, completing the first stitch.

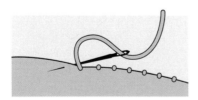

Step 3: Repeat this process for each stitch, using the tip and shank of your appliqué needle to turn under ½-inch-long sections of seam allowance at a time. As you turn under a section, press it flat with your thumb and then stitch it in place, as shown.

PRESSING BASICS

Proper pressing can make a big difference in the appearance of a finished block or quilt top. It allows patchwork to open up to its full size, permits more precise matching of seams, and results in smooth, flat work. Quilters are divided on the issue of whether a steam or dry iron is best; experiment to see which works best for you. Keep these tips in mind:

• Press seam allowances to one side, not open. Whenever possible, press toward the darker fabric. If you find you must press toward a lighter fabric, trim the dark seam allowance slightly to prevent show-through.

• Press seams of adjacent rows of blocks, or rows within blocks, in opposite directions. The pressed seams will fit together snugly, producing precise intersections.

• Press, don't iron. Bring the iron down gently and firmly. This is especially important if you are using steam.

• To press appliqués, lay a towel on the ironing board, turn the piece right side down on the towel, and press very gently on the back side.

ASSEMBLING QUILT TOPS

Lay out all the blocks for your quilt top using the quilt diagram or photo as a guide to placement. Pin and sew the blocks together in vertical or horizontal rows for straight-set quilts and in diagonal rows for diagonal-set quilts. Press the seam allowances in opposite directions from row to row so that the seams will fit together snugly when rows are joined.

To keep a large quilt top manageable, join rows into pairs first and then join the pairs. When pressing a completed quilt top, press on the back side first, carefully clipping and removing hanging threads; then press the front.

MITERING BORDERS

Step 1: Start by measuring the length of your finished quilt top through the center. Add to that figure two times the width of the border, plus 5 inches extra. This is the length you need to cut the two side borders. For example, if the quilt top is 48 inches long and the border is 4 inches wide, you need two borders that are each 61 inches long (48 + 4 + 4 + 5 = 61). In the same manner, calculate the length of the top and bottom borders, then cut the borders.

Step 2: Sew each of the borders to the quilt top, beginning and ending the seams ¼ inch from the edge of the quilt. Press the border seams flat from the right side of the quilt.

Step 3: Working at one corner of the quilt, place one border on top of the adjacent border. Fold the top border under so that it meets the edge of the other border and forms a 45 degree angle, as shown in the diagram. If you are working with a plaid or striped border, check to make sure the stripes match along this folded edge. Press the fold in place.

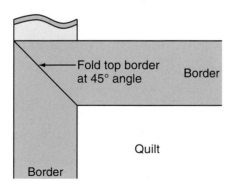

Step 4: Fold the quilt top with right sides together and align the edges of the borders. With the pressed fold as the corner seam line and the

body of the quilt out of the way, sew from the inner corner to the outer corner, as shown in the diagram.

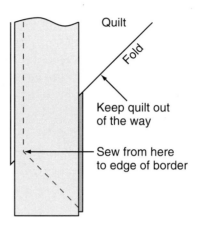

Step 5: Unfold the quilt and check to make sure that all points match and the miter is flat. Trim the border seam allowance to ¼ inch and press the seam open.

Step 6: Repeat Steps 3 through 5 for the three remaining borders.

MARKING QUILTING DESIGNS

To mark a quilting design, use a commercially made stencil, make your own stencil using a sheet of plastic, or trace the design from a book page. Use a nonpermanent marker, such as a silver or white pencil, chalk pencil, or chalk marker, that will be visible on the fabric. You can even mark with a 0.5 mm lead pencil, but be sure to mark lightly.

If you are using a quilt design from this book, either trace the design onto tracing paper or photocopy it. If the pattern will be used many times, glue it to cardboard to make it sturdy.

For light-color fabrics that you can see through, place the pattern under the quilt top and trace the quilting design directly onto the fabric. Mark in a thin, continuous line that will be covered by the quilting thread.

With dark fabrics, mark from the top by drawing around a hard-edged design template. To make a simple template, trace the design onto template plastic and cut it out around the outer edge. Trace around the template onto the fabric, then add inner lines by eye.

LAYERING AND BASTING

Carefully preparing the quilt top, batting, and backing will ensure that the finished quilt will lie flat and smooth. Place the backing wrong side up on a large table or clean floor. Center the batting on the backing and smooth out any wrinkles. Center the quilt top right side up on the batting; smooth it out and remove any loose threads.

If you plan to hand quilt, baste the quilt with thread. Use a long darning needle and white thread. Baste outward from the center of the quilt in a grid of horizontal and vertical rows approximately 4 inches apart.

If you plan to machine quilt, baste with safety pins. Thread basting does not hold the layers securely enough during machine quilting, plus the thread is more difficult to remove when quilting is completed. Use rustproof nickel-plated brass safety pins in size #0, starting in the center of the quilt and pinning approximately every 3 inches.

HAND QUILTING

For best results, use a hoop or a frame to hold the quilt layers taut and smooth during quilting. Work with one hand on top of the quilt and the other hand underneath, guiding the needle. Don't worry about the size of your stitches in the beginning; concentrate on making them even, and they will get smaller over time.

Getting started: Thread a needle with quilting thread and knot the end. Insert the needle through the quilt top and batting about 1 inch away from where you will begin stitching. Bring the needle to the surface in position to make the first stitch. Gently tug on the thread to pop the knot through the quilt top and bury it in the batting.

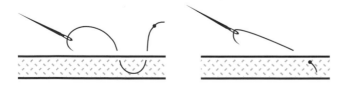

Taking the stitches: Insert the needle through the three layers of the quilt. When you feel the tip of the needle with your underneath finger, gently guide it back up through the quilt. When the needle comes through the top of the quilt, press your thimble on the end with the eye to guide it down again through the quilt layers. Continue to quilt in this manner, taking two or three small running stitches at a time.

Ending a line of stitching: Bring the needle to the top of the quilt just past the last stitch. Make a knot at the surface by bringing the needle under the thread where it comes out of the fabric and up through the loop of thread it creates. Repeat this knot and insert the needle into the hole where the thread comes out of the fabric. Run the needle inside the batting for an inch and bring it back to the surface. Tug gently on the thread to pop the knot into the batting layer. Clip the thread.

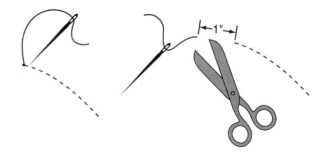

MACHINE QUILTING

For best results when doing machine-guided quilting, use a walking foot (also called an even feed foot) on your sewing machine. For free-motion quilting, use a darning or machine-embroidery foot.

Use thread to match the fabric colors, or use clear nylon thread in the top of the machine and a white or colored thread in the bobbin. To secure the thread at the beginning of a line of stitches, adjust the stitch length on your machine to make several very short stitches, then gradually increase to the regular stitch length. As you near the end of the line, gradually reduce the stitch length so that the last few stitches are very short.

For machine-guided quilting, keep the feed dogs up and move all three layers as smoothly as you can under the needle. To turn a corner in a quilting design, stop with the needle inserted in the fabric, raise the foot, pivot the quilt, lower the foot, and continue stitching.

For free-motion quilting, disengage the feed dogs so you can manipulate the quilt freely as you stitch. Guide the quilt under the needle with both hands, coordinating the speed of the needle with the movement of the quilt to create stitches of consistent length.

MAKING AND ATTACHING BINDING

Double-fold binding, which is also called French-fold binding, can be made from either straight-grain or bias strips. To make double-fold binding, cut strips of fabric four times the finished width of the binding, plus seam allowance. In general, cut strips 2 inches wide for quilts with thin batting or scalloped edges and 2¼ to 2½ inches wide for quilts with thicker batting.

Straight-Grain Binding

To make straight-grain binding, cut crosswise strips from the binding fabric in the desired width. Sew them together end to end with diagonal seams.

Place the strips with right sides together so that each strip is set in ¼ inch from the end of the other strip. Sew a diagonal seam and trim the excess fabric, leaving a ¼-inch seam allowance.

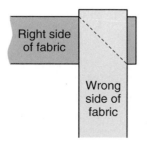

Continuous Bias Binding

Bias binding can be cut in one long strip from a square of fabric that has been cut apart and resewn into a tube. To estimate the number of inches of binding a particular square will produce, use this formula:

Multiply the length of one side by the length of another side, and divide the result by the width of binding you want. Using a 30-inch square and 2¼-inch binding as an example: $30 \times 30 = 900$; $900 \div 2\frac{1}{4} = 400$ inches of binding.

Step 1: To make bias binding, cut a square in half diagonally to get two triangles. Place the two triangles right sides together, as shown, and sew with a ¼-inch seam. Open out the two pieces and press the seam open.

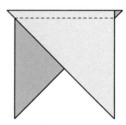

Step 2: Using a pencil and a see-through ruler, mark cutting lines on the wrong side of the fabric in the desired binding width. Draw the lines parallel to the bias edges.

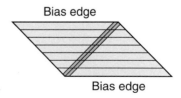

Step 3: Fold the fabric with right sides together, bringing the two nonbias edges together and off-setting them by one strip width (as shown in the diagram at the top of page 122). Pin the edges together, creating a tube, and sew with a ¼-inch seam. Press the seam open.

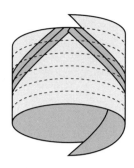

Step 4: Cut on the marked lines, turning the tube to cut one long bias strip.

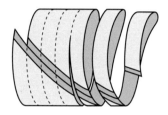

Attaching the Binding

Trim excess batting and backing even with the quilt top. For double-fold binding, fold the long binding strip in half lengthwise, with wrong sides together, and press. Beginning in the middle of a side, not in a corner, place the strip right sides together with the quilt top, align raw edges, and pin.

Step 1: Fold over approximately 1 inch at the beginning of the strip and begin stitching ½ inch from the fold. Sew the binding to the quilt, using a ¼-inch seam and stitching through all layers.

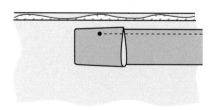

Step 2: As you approach a corner, stop stitching ¼ inch from the raw edge of the corner. Backstitch and remove the quilt from the machine. Fold the binding strip up at a 45 degree angle, as shown in the following diagram on the left. Fold the strip back down so there is a fold at the upper

edge, as shown on the right. Begin sewing ¼ inch from the top edge of the quilt, continuing to the next corner. Miter all four corners in this manner.

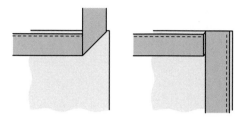

Step 3: To finish the binding seam, overlap the folded-back beginning section with the ending section. Stitch across the fold, allowing the end to extend approximately ½ inch beyond the beginning.

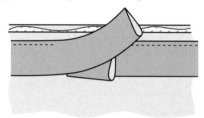

Step 4: Turn the binding to the back of the quilt and blindstitch the folded edge in place, covering the machine stitches with the folded edge. Fold in the adjacent sides on the back and take several stitches in the miter. In the same way, add several stitches to the miters on the front.

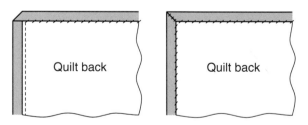

SIGNING YOUR QUILT

Be sure to sign and date your finished quilt. Your finishing touch can be a simple signature in permanent ink or an elaborate inked or embroidered label. Add any other pertinent details that can help family members or quilt collectors 100 years from now understand what went into your labor of love.